BODY BEAUTIFUL

BODY BEAUTIFUL

How Changing the Conversation About Our Bodies Has the Power to Change the World

WORDS + PHOTOS BY GINA D. GRAHAM, LCSW

Publishing support provided by
Ignite Press
5070 N. Sixth St. #189
Fresno, CA 93710
www.IgnitePress.us

ISBN: 979-8-9862331-0-9
ISBN: 979-8-9862331-1-6 (Ebook)

For bulk purchase and for booking, contact:
Gina Graham
GinaMichelleG@icloud.com

Library of Congress Control Number: 2022907602

Cover design by Julie Chen

Edited by Cindy Tschosik and Emma Hatcher

Cover and interior design by Julie Chen

FIRST EDITION

For Danny and Dylan,
may you answer when your heart calls.

"Your body is not your masterpiece.

Your life is."

—GLENNON DOYLE

ENDLESS GRATITUDE

First and foremost, this book could have never happened without the fearless and intrepid courage of the girls and women who were willing to share their stories with us.

To Julie, for starting my engine and for the incredible design work. This book never would have happened without you.

To Vaida, there is an endless list of reasons why I am so grateful to you.

To Ben, who is with me and for me, no matter what, always. It's been such an incredible and bottomless gift.

To Vinnie, my original guru of all things creative.

To my mom, for being my biggest fan, reminding me to dream big, and—basically—everything.

To my dad, who says that I "hung the moon" and believes it, no matter what I say or do.

To my neighborhood tribe, for reading the drafts, giving feedback, and allowing me to push them out of their comfort zones in Michigan.

To Cindy Tschosik, without whose guidance and expertise this book could not have been made. I am sure we were destined to meet at the exact moment that we did.

To Nerija, for your bravery and courage.

To my team at Ignite; Everett, Malia, Emma, and Chris. You all sure do know how to empower and "ignite" a first time author. You are incredible at what you do.

To Rob Bell, who reminded me that underneath this colorful collection of beads is an underlying thread that is me.

To Norma Lynn Higgins, who was my original role model of all that I could become, and who held my hand when I needed it

To the women and girls who have come into my office, trusted me with their hearts and their stories, and allowed me the immense honor of walking a part of their journey beside them.

To Taylor Swift and P!nk, for the endless hours of lyrical inspiration

To Liz Gilbert, Brené Brown, and Glennon Doyle, who blazed the most brazen trail that beckoned me to follow.

CONTENTS

AUTHOR'S NOTE

The following is a body of work created by a white, cis-gendered American woman who has lived within the context of white privilege, socioeconomic privilege, and some degree of thin privilege. This compilation of art, stories, and clinical vignettes in no way means to reduce or oversimplify the conversation around body image as it pertains to complex issues such as eating disorders, oppression, minorities, or any other group. This book is also not designed to impart the critical, evidence-based research that explores a myriad of historical, sociological and biological facets around this topic. Having worked in the field of eating disorders for twenty years, I can assure you that body image issues impact not only those that identify as girls or women but also significantly impact boys, men, non-binary, transgender, and BIPOC communities.

The stories and perspectives shared in this book are my own and those who were brave enough to speak openly with me or allow me to photograph them. I in no way intend to exclude anyone from the conversation, but am only able to share what I have personally experienced and what I have collected up to this point during my work "in the field."

My hopes are for this book to open the conversation so that we can continue to foster dialogue about all of the different ways that cultural messages are directed at subgroups of the population in ways that are harmful. Please be gentle with yourselves, the subjects of this book, and me. I did not set out to write a comprehensive book that touches on body image as it impacts every aspect of our human diversity but rather was inspired to produce a work of my art that I hope helps us to move forward as a collective that honors the life and value of every single human being on this planet.

To your honor,

Gina

Author

MICHELLE OBAMA'S ARMS

introduction

"So, the other day, I was telling my pilates instructor that I want my arms to look like Michelle Obama's arms. That's all I want in life: to have Michelle Obama's arms."

———————————————

In the early hours of the morning, I sat alone in a cafe in Atlanta. The cafe was quiet. It was pretty early, and as usual, I was up at the crack of dawn in search of coffee. I was in town for the weekend to attend a photography conference. The cafe was quiet. I reflected on the new friends I had met who were truly talented in their craft and inspirational in their stories. The weekend had been filled with energy reminiscent of the positive buzzing that happens only in rooms filled with women who are away for the weekend, on fire with passion for living their mission and purpose. My creativity was flowing, my ideas were spinning, and so the quiet morning

1

was a welcome respite to the constant thrum of women feeding off of the electric vibe of the conference.

I sat in this stillness for a few minutes, savoring the first sips of this morning ritual, until the hostess ushered in two women, breaking the silence of the room. As they approached, I heard an uttering of longing from one woman as she walked by my chair to be seated with her friend at a table not far from mine. As they passed, this fragment of conversation was the only audible noise in the room. "All I want in life is to have Michelle Obama's arms," she declared to her friend. I sat with this for a minute, those words hanging in the air, observing those two women. They were middle-aged, like me, and I suspected they were also moms. The badges hanging around their neck announced that they were also conference attendees. And I could tell by the way this conversation was going that at least one of those women didn't like her arms very much.

I thought for a minute about Michelle Obama's arms. I could picture them in the white Jason Wu dress that she wore at the presidential inauguration as her husband, Barack Obama was sworn in as the United States president in 2008. The excitement was palpable as history was being made for the first time, as a black man was elected president of the United States. As ceremonious as inaugurations go, the first lady of the United States stole the national stage as she wore a perfectly fitted dress that highlighted her toned physique. Any woman watching clearly noticed and paid homage to the first lady's "buff bod." It was all the talk. I understood the longing of those women who were desiring Michelle Obama's arms. My arms? Definitely not sculpted.

At first glance, my story is not unlike those other moms. My arms and I have had a fairly complicated relationship. I know that, if I am being honest with myself, I can relate to that woman. I know what it's like to feel like my arms aren't as toned as they could be. To wonder why all that time at the gym didn't seem to be solving the "problem" that was my arms. By now, I have gone far enough into the journey of body image on many levels to know the true impact of these

fleeting and negative thoughts that many women find familiar. So, I steadied my impulse to berate my lack of muscle tone, to plot and plan to resolve the issue, and instead, continued sitting with my coffee and thought about those words hanging in the air.

Their conversation faded from me, and I wondered as I sat there about what their discussion could have sounded like had they not been talking about their bodies.

I'll bet that they were both amazing moms.

I'll bet that they loved their kids so much that it hurt.

I'll bet that they were glad for the weekend break in their endless litany of caretaking and raising of children.

I'll bet that they could have talked all day about those kids, their own fears, and what was on their hearts about motherhood.

I'll bet that they could have talked about their art. Clearly, both were photographers who were in the midst of a weekend chock full of learning, inspiration, and connecting with other enthusiastic and passionate women photographers.

I'll bet that they could have been sharing what they were learning, what drove them to find time amongst their surely over-packed and busy schedules to become better behind the lens.

I'm willing to bet that there is a whole slew of issues, ideas, fears, feelings, and chatter that could have been going down at that table about countless areas of what truly matters in life, the reason that they are here, and who they are here to become.

Instead, they were talking about Michelle Obama's arms. How badly that woman wanted sculpted arms; how badly she felt like she needed them; and how she was so sure that sculpted arms would be the end all be all for her body and in her world.

And I sit here wondering, "Ladies, how did we get here?"

Why is talking about our bodies and the way that we look such a common pastime for women?

The story of women and their relationships to their bodies is not new nor simple. It travels back through the ages. It's steeped in cultural pressures and messages about who women are supposed to be, what they are supposed to do, and—more specifically—how they are supposed to look doing it. Over the years, the cultural expectations have changed a bit. There once was a time that curvy and voluptuous bodies were seen as ideal forms for women: both as a sign of affluence and a symbol of feminine beauty. In the last century, Western culture has seen a shift in the way we portray the "ideal form" for women. The rise of fashion, the beauty industry, the diet and fitness industry, the media, and now, social media have propagated standards that most women desire to meet. Yet few women find that they can achieve goals without taking extreme and even dangerous measures. Over time, the sheer and inescapable force of aging alone places all women who are lucky enough to live a long life in a position to constantly reevaluate who she is, how she looks, and how she measures up to those standards.

Like most of life, the relationship that we have with our bodies is complicated. There are the transgenerational messages that young girls hear about their bodies, passed down from a mother and then her mother before that, "You know that we just have the family hips/lips/ thighs/double chin."

You're familiar with it. It's the dreaded family trait that we hear our parents, aunts, and cousins whisper, giggle, and gasp about during the family gatherings. These discussions are meant to help us relate a shared experience about how we should endure our unique features, shapes, sizes, and weight rather than remind us of a feature that encircles us as a tribe of strong women, complete with the common and intertwined genetics that we each carry.

What is casually said is usually meant to be flippant and disregarded. However, no matter how small the comment, we all truly know that it weaves into and settles somewhere into our mind, psyche, and soul, to be plucked out at the exact moment that the gates of "less-than" open and release a bit of insecurity that has been secretly stored in the depths of our being.

I spoke with Cathy, a friend and fellow therapist about the topic of body image. Cathy shared her thoughts with me: "I feel like [conversation about our bodies is] almost expected or something; like, when women get together, it can feel like, 'Let's start this self-deprecation thing.'

"I think that what we actually say out loud to ourselves and to each other is the tip of the iceberg. It's the conversations that we have quietly amongst ourselves in our own heads that are the whole block of ice that we can't even see. I think that, as women, we have these thoughts in our minds from the moment we wake up until we go to bed. Whether it is, "What am I going to wear?" or "What's going to make me feel good today?" How many times do we change clothes while getting ready for the day because we feel 'fat' in an outfit? I think it's something that dominates 100 percent of our time."

— KATHLEEN, 54

We're just going to get on that train and go with it. And it happens a lot." At sixty-three years old, she expresses feeling like she still hears about it almost constantly amongst her friends. "I have this group of friends, and—to me—they are all rock-star women. They are all gorgeous inside and out. They're attractive, they have these wonderful smiles, and you get this good energy around them. But when we get together, these topics come up every time. Every time. Once it gets started, everyone kind of jumps on the bandwagon."

Cathy also believes that a lot of it has to do with our deep and hard-wired desire for belonging. "I think that there is something about being part of a group; and, once it gets going, everyone just kind of gets on board. I never really know what to say. I want to say, 'You know that you're beautiful' or 'C'mon, ladies!' I find that I just kind of retreat, because it feels toxic to me, even though I could easily get on the same train too. Instead, I just back off and wait for it to pass. It can be so awkward."

As humans, our tribal instincts can—and do—kick in when we are around others, in order to ensure that we feel a part of the group. But it seems that, for girls and women of all ages, to be part of the group means buying in more and more to constant pressures about weight, shape, food, and appearance. Cathy further shares, "Reflecting on how the generations pass, it seems to be getting worse. I think there is a lot of pressure on women now. It's like you have to have a PhD and be a Victoria's Secret model."

Despite these increasing pressures, Cathy hopes that, ultimately, women can relearn how to relate to one another without all the toxic "girl talk." As she put it, "When we get together and start talking like that, it's really boring. It feels like we just go around the room and talk about what we hate about ourselves, what diets we are doing, how much weight we've gained, or what we're eating or not eating. I've been hanging around with these women for years, and now it's kind of turned into this aging thing. Everyone is talking about what they are doing about their skin or wrinkles or which dermatologist they are seeing. The negative conversation about our own bodies is such a downer thing to listen to. I really want to talk about us, our families, our work, or what is happening in our lives."

———————————————

Since I overheard that conversation in the cafe, I sometimes think about the mom I heard wishing that she had Michelle Obama's arms. I wonder if she still talks to her pilates instructor about those arms, and all the things that she wishes she could change about them. I wonder if she deprives herself of things that she enjoys because she thinks that the more she sacrifices, the closer she will be to reach some goal that she has decided is incredibly important to her. I wonder if she even considers that her genetics may naturally prevent her from achieving these "ideal" arms. I wonder if she has daughters who hear her constantly berate her body, talk about being on a diet, and praise herself if she loses a pound in her daily weigh-ins on a scale in her bathroom. I wonder about that mom. And her kids. And the sea of negative messages that they might be swimming in about their bodies.

That sea? About our bodies? What's supposedly "wrong" with our bodies? We are all swimming in it. Which is a shame. Because these bodies—the ones that we all only have one of—they are our only vehicle. Our "ride or die" for all that we hope to accomplish, who we want to be, and what we are here to do during this heartbreakingly short amount of time on the earth.

So, at this point, you must be wondering why I have thought so long and hard about a woman I never officially met who made some offhanded comment in a cafe as she walked by my table. You may be downright curious about why I would carry her words with me in my heart. Why did the comment about Michelle Obama's arms make such an impression on me?

The truth is that I, too, have been in countless conversations like these over the years. There is actually nothing special about comments like that at all. In fact, they are common. So common that we don't even challenge them, question them, or think much about them anymore. I have participated in conversations like these for my entire life. Not long ago, my friends—all beautiful, hardworking, talented women who are killing it in careers and motherhood—took to a group text message to poke fun at our bodies with an assortment of memes, jokes, and self-deprecating comments. It was laughter, banter, and a collective groan about our own bodies. The bodies that birthed our babies. The bodies that carry us through our days. The bodies that house our grief, our dreams, our values, and our souls. The bodies that refuse to stay young and supple and ageless despite all of our best efforts.

The fears and challenges for moms who are raising daughters in this environment are palpable. As an eating disorder clinical therapist for over twenty years, I have been asked time and time again to speak to this issue. Over the years, I have taught parenting groups, participated in interviews, contributed to podcast episodes, and given talks about raising girls with healthy body image. Throughout my work, I have shared what I know, my experiences in working with young girls and women, and how to try to counteract the cultural and societal messages, all the while gently and respectfully inserting the notion that, as parents, it first starts with our own relationships with our bodies and to food at home. So many moms relate to having great concern for their daughters and the perspectives that their girls hold, yet these same moms hold themselves up to some standard or ideal that in some way negates who they are or how they feel about themselves when they look in the mirror.

The other day, I sat at a table amongst friends. One of them, a mom, has an adorable and petite eleven-year-old and mentioned how her daughter weighs herself daily and tries to go days "without eating sugar." Not eating sugar "for days" is a good thing, right? But as we talked, I could tell that this mom was struggling with this. She shared her own tale of a lifetime of body image issues—ones that still plague her.

She knew that she didn't want to inflict and project these issues onto her daughter, but she also wanted her daughter to be "healthy" and "happy with her body" . . . and wasn't sure if that was possible without some of the "intentionality" her daughter was already expressing. When our kids hear us struggling with our own issues of weight and body image, see us weighing

ourselves or complaining about how we look, it gets confusing for them. They hear us talking and see us struggle with these issues ourselves as they simultaneously drink in the tainted water from our society's messages, and yet we tell them they are beautiful and hope that they will hear it.

We've all heard sentiments similar to this one: "I started doing keto. I have already lost six pounds." We've also all heard self-loathing based on diet-related performance: "I have been so bad lately. I need to get back on my diet!" Doesn't it seem like this has become the norm? Isn't this just how girls and women often talk? Whether it's our actual conversations or in our inner narrative, or our "self-talk"; we have language for this. We talk about this. We seem to think about this. A lot.

These conversations: They bother me. They upset me. They come to mind more than I want them to. Why?

I think about it because I have spent most of my life's work as an eating disorder clinical therapist, trying to convince beautiful and talented girls and women to eat and care for their bodies in the most basic way. As in, "If you don't do this, you could die . . ." kind of way.

I think about it because I am also a family photographer who has heard too many requests from moms to "hide" their bodies during a family photoshoot or to photoshop their image later, or who even refuse to get in family pictures at all—because they still have that "last ten pounds" to lose first.

I think about it because I have amazing and talented friends that lament far too often about what is wrong with their bodies.

I think about it because I have far too often sat across from young girls who have overheard their moms talking this way and are now struggling with the messages that they have picked up.

I think about it because I have nieces that I pray daily will know how special and loved they are.

And I think about it because I have spent a lot of time in my own life trying to accept my own body.

My motivation for writing this book is to change the course of the conversation. Culture has done some damage to the psyches of girls and women. I believe that it's time to repair it. There are a lot of things happening in the world, and women are out there doing what we do best: listening, paying attention, nurturing, intuiting, sharing ideas, and creating real change. There is a movement happening in the world that calls for women to rise up, step into their true and radiant power, and be ready and determined to make this world a better place. The rally cry is loud and fierce. We are ready to shake things up, make things happen, and downright run some things. I see it developing, and I am cheering us on and ready to be a part of it. Yet I know that if we don't make it a priority and stop the negative self-talk, we will only get so far. We must stop constantly buying into and believing that something is wrong with our bodies—because when we believe that there is something wrong with our bodies, we believe that there is something wrong with ourselves. And, as a result, we believe that we don't measure up. But right now, women need to know that there is no measure and no limit to what we are capable of doing. And the world needs it too.

So, how do we start? First, we need to recognize that the pressures to conform to body shapes, sizes, and abilities are real, and the struggles seem to grow louder and become more widely accepted by the day. The rise in technology, the fast-paced way of life, and the endless amount of sheer noise that we are all bombarded with is constant. Ladies, we are at war. It is both a silent and not-so-silent war. It is everywhere but so often goes unnamed, unmentioned: an elephant in the room of life. The foot soldiers of this war are so insidious that we have become them. We have turned the weapons on ourselves. The war to claim who we are here to be and step into our power: as of late, we have not been winning that war. It's time to look at our tactics and realize that the enemy is not our own bodies. The last several decades seem to have really cranked up the volume on our narratives.

These narratives run constantly in the way that we talk amongst ourselves.

These narratives need to happen with our daughters, and we are struggling with those conversations.

These narratives run in our minds in the form of constant negative self-talk, comparisons, and put downs: Our bodies. The way they look. How they measure up. What we weigh.

What we eat; what we don't eat; what we want to change—we are already always talking about it. So, let's talk about it for real.

———— LET'S TALK! ————

This collection of stories in this book contains conversations with real women sharing their real stories. It's raw and it's complicated. It's not perfect. It doesn't fit into a neat, little package, and it doesn't all get resolved and wrapped up at the end.

This book speaks to the truthful and ongoing issues that women face in our relationships with our bodies as we go through life, and that reference to women includes me too.

This book expects that we will all continue to struggle with these issues to some degree.

This book asks you to begin to find empathy for yourself and to make a commitment to being kinder to your body, one step at a time.

I'm glad that you have picked up this book. If your heart breaks a little while reading it, then I have done my job. Because how girls and women think about and treat their bodies is, in fact, sometimes heartbreaking. Yet there is hope.

I hope that this book reminds you that, if you relate to these stories in any way, you are not alone.

"I had an eight-year-old tell me how to pose to make my arms look 'skinnier.'"

— TARA, 46

I hope that this book leaves you feeling inspired to take a look at how you talk to and treat yourself.

I hope that this book challenges you to be the best role model that you can be to younger generations of women.

I am proud of you for setting your feet upon this path. Keep walking. The further that we get, the more empowered that we all become. And the more radiant the world will become when we see our own beauty reflected back to us in all that we become and do.

"I believe the biggest challenge that women face today in regard to their body image is keeping up with the impossible standard. This standard is about being a great wife, mother, career woman as well as maintaining our youthful appearance. We hear that staying fit and slim means staying sexy. We hear that spending money on maintaining a youthful appearance will make you more desirable. We have to do it all and be it all while still looking good while doing it."

— CATHERINE, 37

1

SEEDS

"How It All Starts"

"Wide load," two ruthless middle school boys muttered as I weaved between the aisles to the teacher's desk in the front of the room to turn in a paper. On the playground later that fall, one boy spat on me once while making fun of my weight. The irony? He was, by far, one of the heaviest set boys in the grade; thus demonstrating what we all know to be true about the nature of a bully.

In the years before I hit puberty, I struggled with my weight and the teasing was brutal. In spite of being well-liked and a natural leader, some of the boys had been relentless on the playground in grade school and middle school.

It was the late '80s and the social pecking order and the stage were set. MTV exploded onto television sets across America with an endless supply of visual stimuli burned into our synapses to define what girls "should" look like and what they "should" aspire to become. A music video background dancer? Scantily clad video extras?

Teeny bopper shows and teen magazines erupted before our eyes and into our lives, and pop stars became all the rage for young girls. I was no exception. In fact, I loved it! From Daisy Duke to Madonna to Carrie Fisher as Princess Leia in Star Wars, I was all about wanting to be "beautiful." By the time that I reached middle school, I didn't need the boys in the fourth row to inform me that I didn't look like the stars on television. A quick comparison between my body and those I saw in the media made me well aware of the difference between what I saw on television and what I saw in the mirror. And, so it starts: Tiny seeds being planted that can sometimes sprout the negative concept of self that most of us endure at some point in our lives.

As a third-generation Italian immigrant, I was also being raised in a family culture whose traditions cherished and celebrated food. As a young girl, not only did I learn to love food early on, I had also begun to find comfort in food. I began to connect the dots between not feeling good emotionally and swallowing down something that tasted and felt better. And because of all of the yummy brain chemicals that reinforce this behavior, namely dopamine, which is linked to the addiction centers of the brain, it definitely did make me feel better. Often. For the moment anyway.

The truth of the matter was, in middle school, I did weigh more than almost all of the other girls on the playground. My body was growing and changing; and, even before middle school started and much earlier than many of my friends and peers, my body shifted into ground zero for the hormonal revolution of puberty. For young girls going through puberty, it's not uncommon for girls to gain a significant percentage of their fully grown body weight during this time. The other issue complicating this whole thing was the fact that my body was never destined to be tall and thin with lean, perfectly toned muscles. Unbeknownst to me at the time, a very small percentage of the population has a natural body type that lends itself toward the supermodel physique. I was squarely and unequivocally in the other 98 to 99 percent.

Thanks to our genetics, our ability to change our body is more limited than the media and social media outlets lead us to believe. However, for those of us who know our ancestry, it's

easier to gain clues about our natural size and the expected shape of our bodies, especially from the photo archives of our family. The women in my ancestry are memorialized with curves, dark hair, and olive skin—vastly different from the figures that I was seeing glorified in popular culture.

"Skinny" just wasn't in my DNA. By the time I approached middle school, the perfect storm of genetics, puberty, cultural ideals, and a very bad perm raged and rained down upon me until all that was left in its wake was a young girl who had tons of energy, intelligence, creativity, and potential, but felt too big, was uncomfortable with herself, and lacked self-worth.

For millions of American girls, it was impossible to escape thousands of images that flashed throughout media channels every minute across the nation (from magazines to movies) and laid the desire before us to have the "ideal body." This was an alarming set up for any one of us who presumably failed at matching the demands of American media, advertising, and entertainment empires.

Looking back, I can see the ways that my mom had tried to help me with my early onset of body image issues. My mom was no stranger to diet and body talk. The women in her generation had all been raised by the women in the prior generation as denoted on the higher limbs of the family tree. And they all understood the modicum to be pleasing to the eye as part of the gig for the 1950's and 1960's housewives.

Moms in the late '80s were raised by women who had begun to create real momentum for the beauty and fashion industries in the boom of the post-war era. The '80s and '90s were also a time of exploding fitness and diet culture, with the burgeoning of highly processed, low-fat foods, allowing diet behavior to seep into daily lives under the guise of being "for our health." At the time, I felt like a girl whose body spilled out of the tiny container that it was "supposed" to fit in. And my mom, who loved me so much, was willing to do anything to take away my pain. Now I'm a mom and know all too well the lengths that we will go through to help our kids with issues that they truly feel helpless about.

In retrospect, I can see times where both of my parents were, in some way, focused on their weight. Add to that my own increasing size and weight during puberty, and we began to talk more about what we were eating. The media at that time was hyping all of these new diets, and so we did what everyone is told by our culture to do: We went on a diet. We joined the bandwagon of the low-fat food craze. Diet foods appeared in the house. Exercise equipment was provided. Discussion at the family dinner table occasionally started to veer away from what was happening in our lives and more toward what was or wasn't on our plates. Over time, my body did begin to change as a direct result of exercising more, being involved with sports, and in general, paying more attention to what was going into my mouth.

But my body was also just going through the normal and healthy process of puberty and maturation. Over time, it began to balance itself out a bit more. Slowly, over time, I did start to shed some of the pounds that had come along for the ride in middle school. I just didn't notice. I couldn't notice. Seemingly, somehow, my body image issues had become a bit stuck. The version of myself in the mirror didn't accurately reflect back to me how I really looked. In my mind's eye, I had created this fixed and permanent version of myself. And that girl, I was telling myself, was "large, fat, too big, and not thin enough." The fact that my body was changing in response to healthier eating habits and increased physical activity did not register in the mirror, in my self-talk, or in my beliefs, in spite of my relatively average size, shape and weight. No, I didn't look like those 1990's supermodels. But I was growing and developing, my body was becoming my own. I was becoming "me-shaped."

By the time I reached high school, I found myself at the doorway of the Jenny Craig© Weight Loss Center, not knowing that there was nothing wrong with my body. Sadly, it wasn't until much later that I got the memo.

Today, we are seeing body image disturbance in young girls as early as eight or nine years old. However, it mostly starts to impact girls around ten to eleven years old, when they become more aware of their body in relation to the world around them.

"I get uncomfortable because I am taller than people. I'm actually the tallest in the school, and it's not the one that I want to be. It makes me stand out, and I don't like to stand out."

— ELLA, 12

As a therapist, when I ask a little girl what she likes about her body, I usually get a blank stare. Girls that are young generally don't even think about their bodies as separate from themselves. They are just in their bodies. It doesn't occur to them to objectify it. That comes later.

Young girls are blissfully unaware that their thoughts and beliefs about their bodies can become detached from the reality of who they are intrinsically. When I clarify the question, young girls often tell me mostly about what their bodies do for them. Seven-year-old Maria responds, "I like that I can ride a bike. I like that I can climb things at the park." In relation to their bodies, girls this age often tell me about the sports they like to play and the way that their bodies move in the world to accomplish something that is meaningful for them. "I like that I know how to fight. Well, at least my older sister," laughs Alice at age nine. Generally, though, there is still little connection to the way their bodies look. Anyone who is older than a tween might struggle to appreciate their body abilities as much as five-year-old Summer, "I like my body because I can do tricks. I can make funny sounds and words. I like it when I lose my teeth. It's so much fun."

And it is fun. Until slowly, insidiously, over time, something shifts. Like a slow bleed.

Something begins to erode.

When I ask a teenager what she likes about her body, I usually get a blank stare. It doesn't occur to them to like their bodies all that much, including Emily who is fourteen years old. "At one point I really wanted to be famous, but then I thought about it. I felt like, 'This would tear me apart.' I would always have to be doing something for someone. I would always have to be 'perfect.' I would always be telling myself, 'I should': 'I should try to be skinny' and 'I should try to be pretty.' Honestly, I don't think I'm pretty, but I'm okay with that. I feel like I have really fat and clumpy legs, and it bothers me."

Something has changed. The little girl who once celebrated what her body could do and what was fun about living in her body has now grown up and become someone else. By this point, girls have generally lost the ability to think about their bodies without the filter of how it looks. How it measures up. It's as if that little girl who once celebrated that she could run and jump and climb has altogether forgotten that she can run and jump and climb. For a lot of teens, the idea that their bodies are here for a reason other than how it looks is just as mind boggling as it is to her younger self understanding the concept that her body is even a separate topic to be discussed and dissected.

Messages to young girls about weight, shape and appearance can come from a lot of places. The more we have looked at this phenomenon over the years, the more we see the breathtaking impact on girls and women's self-esteem, body image, and self-worth that is the direct blow from cultural ideals, societal pressures, and unrealistic beauty standards. Society and these messages are an easy culprit to blame. The overarching presence of it is so pervasive that it has become a widely accepted cultural norm. A vibrant and lovely fifteen-year-old told me that she doesn't feel beautiful, even though her mom tells her all the time that she is. What's a mom to do? I know these moms. I talk to these moms. They are a constant and ever-present, steady voice in their daughter's ears as they head out into the world:

You know that you are beautiful, inside and out, right?

But it falls on deaf ears. It can't compete with the sheer noise of media, social media, diet culture, and the day to day "chatter" about our bodies. These moms feel defeated. Deflated. When it comes to media and culture, for so many parents, it can feel like a battle that they can't win, and they know it. It can feel like showing up to a gunfight with a butter knife, dead on the spot before you can even come close to engaging the enemy.

———————————————

Messaging directed to women about their bodies spans all cultures, races, ages, and societal norms. A common misconception in our culture is that body image issues mostly affect only young, white girls. But in talking to women of all ages, races, and cultural backgrounds, it becomes evident that the predominant worry about the body and physical appearance can last a lifetime.

Women of color have also experienced confusion and stress around their bodies and the way they look. Patricia remembers having a lot of angst while growing up and being told that she had to look a certain way and act a certain way. As a black woman, she realizes now that those ideals were not realistic for black females, because their body frames are completely different from other ethnicities. Adding more confusion to their perspective was the fact that, while Patricia was growing up, they didn't see black women on television or in magazines very much, so there wasn't anyone with a similar genetic background for them to emulate. Today is a bit different, because she can encourage her daughter to follow celebrities on social media who have a healthy outlook and take care of their bodies.

In Latina culture, the struggles continue even well into adulthood, too, as Elena, at forty-three years old, is still uncomfortable accepting compliments. "My perception of me is that I am not beautiful. There is an expectation that women should be curvy, and growing up, I didn't have any of that. I still don't to this day. It's not my natural body type. When I was a little girl, I was called flaca, which in Spanish means 'skinny.' I hadn't grown into my body and didn't get breasts until later, so I felt like boys weren't going to look at me. The other nickname that I had was fea which means 'ugly.' I think that back then, my family members didn't realize how much it affected me and how much the teasing nicknames made an impact. Because of it, I always felt like 'the ugly duckling.' Over the years, that really stuck with me. To this day, it's still hard to accept compliments about my physical appearance."

Marisol, a thirty-seven-year-old Latina agrees with Elena, "Something that has been profound for me is that there is a lot of emphasis on beauty with being a Latina. There's pressure to be 'a beautiful Latina who has a curvaceous body.' They are supposed to be exotic and beautiful. Curvaceous, with a little waist. For Latina women there is this message that it's okay to have

"I do think that there is a pressure to look a certain way. I think that a lot of girls I know spend alot of time in the morning trying to figure out what they are going to wear, how they are going to do their hair, and how they are doing their makeup. I don't really care that much. Personally, I like to look good, but I don't really feel the pressure of someone trying to make me into who I'm not."

— ISABELLA, 12

'extra,' as long as it's in the 'right places.' These are things that are so challenging to navigate, and it has been such a part of my journey."

In talking to women from Southeast Asian and Muslim cultures, the confusion and messaging is also a factor when it comes to girls and women relating to their bodies through the lens of their predominant values. This is especially true for girls and women whose families emigrate to Western countries where the cultures quickly clash.

Kashvi was born in The United States, but her parents are from India and have raised her with predominant values and ideals from their native land. Kashvi, who is twenty-three years old, shares how body image, mental health, and expectations for women aren't overtly talked about, but are still driving women's beliefs and behaviors. "Indian culture doesn't really talk about body image a lot. In our culture, we don't bring it up much, and it's very subtle. Indians can be very blunt about what they say when they do talk about it. In my experience, Indian people never believed in eating disorders, anxiety, or depression. I think my parents have started to become more educated about these issues. These things are real. A lot of Indian parents will compare their daughter's bodies to others or have a standard of needing to be 'skinny.' In our outfits, we show a lot of skin, and if you're not thin, then it feels like the outfits of our culture don't fit you and aren't made for you. It's sad because women in our culture can feel less comfortable and less happy on their wedding day and on special occasions."

As a Muslim, Muna also shares the confusion in straddling two cultures, while at the same time trying to understand her relationship to her own body. At twenty-four-years-old she eloquently explains, "Cultural messages have impacted me twofold as a child of immigrants who are Muslim. I've had to experience two different cultural views on body and beauty, both damaging yet both also empowering in different senses. At times, my two cultures would be saying opposing messages, leaving me confused on what beauty standards to hold myself to. In the end, I've learned to take the good from both the American and Somali cultures and redefine what it means to me."

The cultural confusion, as well as the lack of representation, celebration, and acceptance of all sizes, races, and ages in media are absolutely at the root of body image and self-worth issues for many girls and women. But our relationships to our bodies are complex and multi-faceted. A dizzying number of factors play out over time that build stories and core beliefs. These stories and core beliefs are often not generated in just one particular way. Without a doubt, the cultural messages and pressure from media, social media, socioeconomic privilege, and the beauty and fashion industry are an undeniable force of negativity for girls and women in regards to body image and self-esteem. But we also can't talk about the issue without first honestly and compassionately acknowledging that sometimes, some of these stories are passed down through the generations, from one mom to her little girl, to the next. When I talk to those moms, I hear that those stories are often in some way passed down from their moms. On and on it goes, creating a vicious cycle of women who love their daughters, but are so swept up in their own issues, fears, and insecurities that they pass down toxic messages, often without even realizing it.

When I first met Madison in my office, she was a freshman in college. She had big dreams to impact the world with her work in a big way. When talking to Madison that first day, it became clear that her dream was quickly being sabotaged by a new dream; to be thin at all costs. Her diet turned into a full-fledged problem during that first year away from home. She couldn't concentrate. She couldn't focus. Partly because she wasn't eating enough. And partly because all she could think about was how uncomfortable she felt in her body and how badly she wanted to lose weight. She weighed herself constantly, only to be discouraged and depressed each day that the number on the scale didn't go down. These problems weren't necessarily new. Madison had struggled her entire life to feel like her body was "good enough." Unbeknownst to her, her mother had had the same issues.

31

Struggling with her own body image, Madison's mom lost a lot of weight in college and found herself bound up by intense food rules in order to maintain that body. Looking back at this time, she acknowledges that she was "basically anorexic for a while." Throughout adulthood, Madison's mom was careful not to buy any "junk food" and weighed herself often. As Madison grew up, she began to notice that the household foods she was used to were different from those of her friends and peers. She noticed that she was not allowed to have chips or treats in her lunch, when her friends at school often did. She noticed that she was not allowed to request that her mom buy certain food items because they weren't healthy.

Because of the "dangerous" nature of these foods, Madison's family began to have this unspoken belief that it was actually "safer" to have these foods out of the house.

During a meeting in my therapy office, we revealed that at some point, the women in the house had all made a silent agreement of sorts to exclude "off-limits" foods in the pantry, for fear of losing control and eating too much. "Better to just not buy it." Any "junk food" that did find its way into the house was hidden away. Like a dirty little secret, food was stashed in so many places of the house, that Madison's mom had lost track of where it all was hidden. It had become a running joke in the family, an accepted eccentricity. The women in the family both did, and yet didn't, think that it was a bit strange. As we all sat and talked, it was apparent that both generations of women in this family struggled to trust that they could enjoy all foods in moderation without bingeing or overeating. Within a few weeks of that meeting, Madison was headed back to college, an environment rife with conversations and pressures about weight and appearance.

Within a month of being back on campus, Madison was struggling. Even with an active social life, supportive friends, school clubs, and a challenging course load, she could not stop thinking about weight loss. She just couldn't shake the feeling that her weight and shape were the primary reasons she felt so unhappy, depressed, and anxious. In her mind, if only she could "fix" the issue of her weight, she could finally be happy. With this belief firmly rooted and in place,

"My relationship with my body is horrible. I do not like how I look. No matter what people say that's positive, I do not feel that way at all."

— MOLLY, 11

it's no wonder why she was struggling to focus on anything else. There was talk of bringing her home to get mental health treatment and be supervised with her eating. And of course, her mom was intensely worried.

This girl. This Mom. My heart hurt for them. This trap is so common.

In Madison's case, there were a lot of pieces to the puzzle of why she was struggling, including hormonal imbalances, medical issues, and biochemical depression. To pinpoint the family eating habits as the sole cause of Madison's problem would be a grave oversimplification and an incomplete and incorrect explanation. But still, the reality is that learned patterns and beliefs about food and weight from within our own households can have negative effects that are often not intended but there, nonetheless.

These women have similar experiences to so many families. All of them "knowing" what they think they "know" about food, weight, and body image—"Junk food is bad." Or "Losing weight and being small is good." That so-called "knowing," however, is often a hodgepodge of diet myths, powerful and negative messages about women's bodies, and transgenerational insecurities.

For better or for worse, a mother's relationship to herself is one of the most incredibly powerful forces of modeling for a daughter or girl to see while growing up. Moms can't hide their issues with their bodies for long. A mother's negative talk, behaviors, and emotions about her own body seeps into the foundation of things, in spite of all attempts to hide it or deny it. Often a daughter's need for help with positive body image is a signal that the family may need help with developing a more positive outlook on body image as well. The seeds that are planted and take root for girls and women that their bodies are a "problem" to be fixed at all costs come from many directions. The beliefs and messages to girls and women run wide and deep. Most of it comes from centuries of historical objectification of women, their place in society, and the degree to which they measure up to an unrealistic set of standards aimed to sell them things at least or keep them in a disempowered place at its worst.

Which parts of these stories and experiences can you relate to?

———————————————— LET'S TALK! ————————————————

How often do you find yourself talking about your body, food, and weight? Pay attention and create some awareness of what you think, say, do, and feel.

When do you become aware of these negative conversations? Write them down, and then commit to shut them down!

Remember to pay attention to both of your internal and external conversations.

Think like a "little girl!" Put your focus and your attention on what your body does for you!

When you get caught in negative thinking about the appearance of your body or a particular body part, focus on gratitude, instead. Write down or say thank you for a particular movement or action that your body can do with that body part.

If you are a parent or live with younger girls, don't be afraid to have honest and open discussions at home about your own struggles with your body and body image. Remember you can't truly hide it.

Create new conversations at home that debunk the cultural messages about food and weight.

Do all that you can to stop the cycle of transgenerational body image "hang-ups."

Assess honestly and with loving kindness whether or not any family member needs help in role modeling better body image at home.

Compliment others based on things other than weight and appearance. Love their creativity? Think they did a great job in a game or at work? Share your praise without making it about weight, shape, or looks.

2

UNFOLLOWING

"Social Media"

"It's not you, it's me." That's how I felt when I unfollowed one of the most prolific, and admittedly seemingly nicest interior designers on social media. By now, this designer is a household name in America, and has officially blossomed in the fertile soil and cultural landscape of aspirational popular culture. To the observing eye, she has "made it" and arrived in every way. I first fell in love with her and her life while watching her very popular renovation show on television. I was enchanted. I was enthralled. I realized, though, that I was beginning to feel wildly inadequate. It all seemed so effortless for her. Homemade muffins on a Saturday morning cozied up with my family by the fire? Sure, I wanted that. Instead, I was running around, hair-on-fire, juggling kids' soccer schedules, photo shoots, and gulping down coffee along the way.

What began to bother me the most while following along with her "life" was a haunted feeling like I was not the mother that I wanted to be. Sometimes, I would scroll through her online content. I felt a chasm of longing for her idealized version of the type of motherhood that doesn't look like my life. When I repeatedly found myself feeling this way, I knew it was time to stop scrolling and unsubscribe from her page. The reason why I started to need distance from this content? I was forgetting to see that her curated and highly produced version of "life" was this woman's job. I failed to see the teams and staff that it took to create this content that was shared with the world in the hopes of creating inspiration and aspiration for a "life." Instead, I had forgotten that it is no way an accurate representation of my life. While following her, I was not privy to her own issues and insecurities. I was not privy to her marital struggles, her parenting struggles, and all the balls she drops in this great juggling act known as motherhood. I did not see the ways she, too, feels guilty, and I'm sure, sometimes, feels like a failure as a mother. Don't we all? All I saw was slick perfection, beauty and the stuff of Pinterest-worthy dreams. It didn't really look like my life, and the way it's depicted online probably isn't hers either. And in failing to see that and getting swept up by the intoxication of it all, I was left with an icky, achy feeling that I wasn't doing enough, being enough, and wasn't enough.

In my therapy practice, I call this issue "Compare and Despair." It happens at any age, as indicated by what Grace, who is twelve, shares, "I sometimes see myself in comparison to people I see at school or on YouTube. I wonder sometimes why I couldn't have been born blonde. I know a lot of pretty girls that are blonde. Also, I always compare my eyes to theirs. They have blue eyes or pretty green or hazel eyes, and mine are brown. I always wonder why I had to come out really, like, plain. I would say I look 'ordinary' and 'nothing special.' "

Holding ourselves up to these external "realities," we are often left feeling negative, down, and with a general lack in our own lives in some form or another. A woman younger than me living on a farm in another part of the country with a team of people at her disposal is not the same as me living my life in the suburbs of a large city with an entirely different life, job and situation. We all fall prey to this belief on social media that all things are created equal, when, in reality,

we are all our own unique and complex blends of our own realities. The very act of comparing pits one thing against the other. One wins, the other loses. The nature of it all is to judge and deem one as better than or less than. It isn't fair and it doesn't do justice to the beautiful and diverse lens in which we all deserve to see ourselves and one another.

We all want to be seen and heard in our lives. We all crave connection and belonging. It is hardwired into our DNA. Some of us quite literally have a deep and intense need to have a platform, to share, to be vocal. For some people, sharing, using their voice, and connecting with others is very much a part of their purpose. For others, yes, it can be an attention-seeking attempt to fill a gaping hole in the heart where self-affirmation should squarely sit. Fortunately, Elyse, a fourteen-year-old girl, expressed having a positive experience with Snapchat. "I feel like Snapchat actually helped me because I have more friends now. Now I am more connected. I am not insecure anymore because all my friends on Snapchat support each other, and I don't feel like we are trying to drag each other down. I am very happy with the friends I have online. They are nice to me."

Either way, it all stems from the place that is hardwired into us to belong and to feel validated. And yes, social media can be a misplaced place to try to fill that need. As for the effects of this on our pre-teens and teens, the alarm bells are officially going off for almost every parent.

In terms of body image, we don't need to dive too deep to see how media, social media, and the messages that women get about how they are supposed to look and who they are supposed to be can affect girls and women on many levels. A celebrity's public image is often a combination of behaviors, looks, and lifestyle. It's inextricably intertwined and woven into a mixture of extreme diets, extreme workouts, and the lifestyle that comes with having endless amounts of money and an entire team or "glam squad." For girls who are asking that eternal and ever-present question of "How do I compare?"—it can be a minefield. Subsequently, questions sprout from their minds like weeds in spring:

"Am I like that?"

"Why don't I look like that?"

"What does it say about me if I don't look or act like that?"

For a pre-teen or a teenager to look at and compare herself to a fully developed, often digitally or surgically altered version of an older girl or woman is a complete set up for failure. But these girls are not just comparing themselves to celebrities. While scrolling social media, young girls are endlessly appraising how they stack up even against their own friends.

Ava is effervescent. She is fifteen and full of life. When she laughs, it sounds like bells. Her smile is absolutely contagious. Ava is being raised in a home focused on faith and family values. A tight-knit and mixed-race clan, her family loves bike riding, taking "epic adventures," and spending time together. As she is one of several athletes in the family, there is a focus on health and wellness for athletic performance and overall life-balance. In spite of this tremendous foundation, social media and the media has thrown a lot at her that she is actively trying to work out for herself. Ava can now talk openly about how she has had to figure out some matters regarding her cultural background, growing up loving comic books, and the myriad of ways that society has tried to tell her who to be, no matter how many times her parents told her often that she is beautiful inside and out.

"My mom has always told me that I'm beautiful, but for the longest time I didn't believe her. I grew up on comic books. I am a huge fan. Comic book heroines have a butt, they have huge boobs, and then they have a tiny waist. I remember going through puberty and thinking, 'my body is supposed to look like that.' But that was a point of reference that I had. I started to think about my body and realized that I didn't have those curves."

By the time she was in eighth grade, Ava had what she describes as "body image issues." Slowly, though, over time, she began to question what she was seeing in pop culture. She described looking at images of models and celebrities and beginning to question the message that

"I had social media during some of fifth, sixth, and seventh grades, but it started to bother me. My parents took it away from me, and at first, it made me mad. But then I realized that I was a happier person without it. I started putting my phone down more. I just think it's better for me because then I enjoy more moments in life."

— LAUREN, 13

she was being forced to swallow; "I started looking at the models and I was telling myself, 'They just aren't healthy.' I realized that I could outrun them. I could beat them up, to be honest. Now, today, I don't have as many body issues. I don't have a thigh gap. So what? The girls that do have a thigh gap can't run as fast or as hard as I can."

By the way, a "thigh gap" is a big deal for girls today. Pop culture has impressed upon girls that "ideal legs" are when a female stands with their ankles and knees together and there is a space at the top of the leg in between the legs where the thighs don't touch, thus having a "thigh gap." It is a dangerous and toxic ideal, and many of my ED (eating disorder) clients talk about it and explain, "It's a body goal."

When asked specifically about how she started to turn the tide of negative self-talk and comparison on social media, Ava changed who and what she follows online which has been tremendously helpful. She admitted that she still has to be mindful of some content on her feed, "I follow some people who I know are young and have tons of plastic surgery, so I keep that in mind. I remind myself that their bodies aren't natural; they've been photoshopped, or they've had plastic surgery. Most of my feed is, honestly, just athletes, so I think that helps a lot. I don't really follow a ton of influencers. I mostly follow steeplechasers, rock climbers, and female athletes."

Ava is working on achieving a better relationship with her body and social media networks and admits she still struggles from time to time. "I don't think that my body issues have gone away. I just have come to accept them. But there are times that I feel confident. I feel the most confident after track practice. It feels good and satisfying. Exercise makes me happy. It's not just to look good. It makes me feel good."

When it comes to her accepting her cultural heritage, Ava now honors how her body was genetically designed. "People's bodies are so different. I've been looking at my mom and dad and their families. I've realized that I'm never going to have a six pack and huge boobs, because that doesn't run in my family. Even if I had everything I wanted, I feel like it still wouldn't be "good enough," so why feel bad about myself all the time? There will always be a flaw. My body is my body. This is what I can do with it. I am proud of what I can do with it. This is my genetic heritage from my ancestors."

When asked, many girls like Ava can recognize that what they are seeing on social media and in culture isn't "real." But for so many girls and women, this is a constant challenge to remember while they spend hours a day aimlessly scrolling. In the early 2000's, in my therapy office, I was having a hard time convincing young girls that the images they were seeing in the media were "airbrushed, not real, and photoshopped to the hilt." I knew what was happening. I tried to provide evidence of it, but my clients weren't buying it, convinced that there were many women walking around in the world looking exactly like they did on the billboards, and that, if they just worked hard enough at it, they could too. In my office now, despite the fact that most girls and women have the tools and the knowledge to alter an image of themselves within seconds, there is still doubt and confusion about the degree to which media outlets are altering original images.

In 2004, before social media was a prolific fixture in the lives of girls and women, the Dove Advertising Campaign shocked the world by trying to sell soap using "real women" in their underwear rather than airbrushed, thin models. The women on the billboards, for the first time, reflected back the reality of most women's bodies. Photographed in only undergarments, the photos revealed stretch marks, tummy rolls, lumps, and bumps. At the time, this ad campaign was both praised and shamed. It created an ongoing controversy about whether or not the viewers felt validated by the campaign or felt that Dove was just one more company trying to sell products to women by manipulating their psyches and playing on their fears and insecurities. And the question was raised about whether or not celebrating beauty at all in regard to outward physical appearance is further damaging and demoralizing women.[1][2]

Enter social media, and, seventeen years later, The Dove Campaign is alive and well, still trying to illuminate the discrepancy between perfectly airbrushed marketing campaigns and real consumers on the street and IRL (in real life). The Dove Campaign has made it a company mission to continue to try to educate girls and women. The research team at Dove surveyed 556 girls between the ages of ten to seventeen, and recently found that "one in three girls don't think they look good without photo editing." Dove also estimates that 80 percent of girls are using photo retouching apps by the age of thirteen. In response to these statistics, Dove is currently asking girls and women on social media to pledge to stop using digital distortion with images posted online and has launched a full-scale effort to celebrate bodies of all colors, shapes, and sizes—complete with birth marks, stretch marks, scars, and other "issues." Because of this current cultural trend to predominantly post images that have been tweaked, altered, or tuned, the sad reality for our girls—and even older women—is that seeing a "real" picture of our "real" selves online is not only unexpected but also causes shame and negative self-talk. It's almost creating a culture where our actual physical faces and bodies are becoming intolerable.[1][2][3]

For parents, the rising number of preteens and teens who seem to fail to grasp the sheer power of social media is terrifying. And with good reason. From a psychosocial and developmental perspective, no one is more susceptible to the need to "fit in" than adolescents. Most of them engage in constant access to cell phones, complete with an endless array of social media apps that we parents can hardly keep up with or fully understand. As adults, a lot of us seem to understand that an over-identification with our public personas and personal pages is not really where we should focus an intense amount of time and energy. However, the temptation to be scrolling without proper boundaries can still be a slippery slope, even for many adults and parents.

———————————————

Jessica, now in her mid-thirties, tells me that social media in adulthood has changed the way that she sees herself. "When I was a kid, I had very high self-esteem. But because of social media, I now feel worse about my body at thirty-five, which is when I should like it. My body has done cool stuff. I gave birth to two children. I should like it more than I do right now. If I look at it objectively, I have been hitting all kinds of achievements with my body, and I want to say thank you to it, but it's tough."

"I think a lot of the pressure is from each other. Classmates try to outdo each other or look as good as 'so and so.' But since TikTok and social media, everyone is following people in the movie or music business and celebrities. I think that they look up to them a lot. I think that people seeing the staged lives makes them want to have the same thing."

— HANNAH, 12

After the birth of her second child, Jessica started working out at a local gym and fell in love with the rowing machine. Due to having two daughters close together in age, Jessica hadn't exercised regularly for about five years and found that, through this new experience with fitness and her body, she "loved being able to achieve things on the rower that [she] didn't know was possible." As she further expressed, "With rowing, there are all of these milestones you can hit on this machine. There is a whole community to check stats, do time trials, and try to hit certain rankings. It's been a way to prioritize myself and prioritize time for myself. I'm a beginner, but I realized that I could hit a million meters, and that became this realistic goal, given my abilities. And now I'm really close."

When asked about how her newfound love of the sport has impacted her body image, Jessica tells me, "It makes me feel pretty powerful. It makes me feel like I am capable. I had never played sports as a kid. I think that to achieve something like this is really different for me, and it makes me feel really good. My body is definitely changing, and I have muscles in places that I've never had. It's been a fun experience, and it's going to be a big milestone for me."

While there is a lot of newfound appreciation for what her body can do, Jessica acknowledges that there are still significant struggles.

At a recent family event, Jessica had a hard time with a photograph that was taken during the day: "I had someone take a family photo at my daughter's first birthday. I felt like I had this tummy roll around my waist, and I was so unhappy with that picture. Which is a bummer, because that's the only picture we have from that event."

Jessica is open with the fact that, at this stage in her life, she finds both medication and therapy to both be helpful in managing her emotional well-being. And while medication has improved her mood and outlook, Jessica has dealt with the frustrating side effect of weight gain and found herself focusing on the number on her scale more than she would like to. "I started to realize in therapy the importance of looking at my triggers with my body image. I work out six days a week. I move a lot, and it's discouraging to see the scale continuing to creep up. I don't think it's an obsession, but I started weighing myself more often. So, I moved the scale out of the bedroom, because it was just not working for me. It just isn't a good representation of my health. I think that made me realize that the behavior of weighing myself daily had to go. And I do feel a little bit better."

Jessica is also learning in therapy the degree to which social media is a trigger for her. "I make a point on social media to follow body-positive accounts. I want to follow only women who embrace their body or maybe who are my size or bigger. But I sort of realized that even those women are presenting very polished fronts for their accounts. Even though they talk about not wearing makeup or whatever, to me, they still look 'perfect.' It started to feel kind of damaging. I had begun to rely on those accounts to put me in a better headspace, and it wasn't happening. I started to really challenge even the women saying they were looking like "regular women." I started having to delete a lot of accounts.

In addition to deleting accounts, Jessica finds that setting limits and finding alternative activities has helped. "I do try to limit my time on social media as much as possible. I make a lot of goals every year, and one of them this year was to pick up my book more instead of picking up my phone. That has helped with becoming more aware of it when I'm scrolling. I work on mindfulness a lot in therapy, and it's really difficult for me, but it does help. It just sometimes feels like too much, and I unfollow accounts that don't make me feel good."

But maybe it's not all entirely bad news. When it comes to social media and media, the reality is that it's not going anywhere, mainly because in addition to being truly addictive, it is also so profitable to so many. One client of mine used Instagram (a platform that currently is full of body positive accounts, if you look for them) to promote her love of fashion and her fuller body type. She found the experience of finding her voice, advocating her beliefs, and putting herself "out there" to be empowering on many levels. Seen through this lens, social media can indeed be a place that can be used for good. The reality is that—in spite of all of the trolling, negativity, and misinformation—social media has also been a springboard of social justice, social reform, and social movements. Many groups with well-intentioned aims are being born and bred on social media.

"Sometimes when people are hating, I just sing the famous Taylor Swift song 'Shake It Off' in my head. We know the haters will hate, and I feel better when I shake it off," eight-year-old Anna explained. Is it possible to separate the wheat from the chaff when it comes to social media consumption? To have some kind of balance that needs constant tweaking and vigilance but still reaps some positive purpose? Everyone needs to listen to their own guidance and instinct, but I say, "Yes. Of course, with the caveat to always be careful, assess how you are really feeling, and focus on real life in the real world first." I truly believe that a rock-solid survival strategy is needed to engage in social media. Some top tactics for navigating social media in a healthy manner include knowing when to take a break, setting limits, and focusing solely on being a positive and creative force for the good of others. It can also include following only people that you know and love or who inform and inspire you in positive ways. This requires a ruthless editing process and a mindful approach. It requires you to recognize that twinge inside that you feel when you look at someone else's content and begin to feel something stir inside of you that in any way, shape or form makes you feel bad about yourself. It means not consuming. Not exposing yourself. Not following. That might even include that sweet, little, interior designer the whole world loves and adores for all the right reasons.

——————————— LET'S TALK! ———————————

Remember that comparing your life on social media to the lives of others often leads to negative feelings. You never know the "behind the scenes" of the way that things are portrayed on social media. Often, content is photoshopped, falsified, or simply a distorted slice of their "reality."

Develop a confident strategy for social media. Remember that your worth and value are not tied to the number of likes, comments, and followers.

Post proudly and move on! Try not to circle back to check in on how it was received.

See it as a platform to show up and serve up something positive and meaningful.

See it as an opportunity to be creative.

Constantly curate, tweak, and reevaluate your feed and your content. Delete things that bug you, make you feel bad about yourself, or that you find yourself comparing yourself to.

Find positive role models. Follow accounts of strong, confident women that you admire beyond the way that they look. Follow body positive accounts, strong female athletes, or women entrepreneurs. Positive role models on social media are out there. You just need to find and follow them.

Know when to step away and take breaks. Create limits. We all need them. Each and every one of us.

Shut out the critics! Someone trolling you online? Block them. Report them.

Don't let ignorant and unkind words have power over you.

Struggling with something someone said about you online? Find someone you trust to talk about it right away.

Pledge to not distort bodies and faces using filters, tuning apps, or other apps that alter digital images. Talk to girls about whether or not they are comfortable posting a "real" image of their face or body—one without a filter.

"I think social media has a huge, huge impact on younger women and how they eat. What about all of these little kids that are so easily influenced by these celebrities that are pushing coffee diets, negative talk, and plastic surgery? I think that people can use social media as a way to dwell on their bodies and it becomes a constant cycle."

— ELLEN, 25

3

SOPHIA SAYS

"A Story of Adolescence"

"It's almost like our brains are trained to think 'I'm not good enough. I need to look better.' I feel like that's always going to be my first instinct. That's when I know that I need to use logic and think about everything my body does for me."

Sophia, age seventeen, is a breath of fresh air. Sophia is the young woman involved at school and volunteering for special needs. The young woman at the Women's March speaking out on issues important to her. To the casual observer, it would seem as if she had things all figured out by her senior year of high school. But for Sophia, there were a few bumps in the road of adolescence and some struggles that she still wrestles with as she prepares to head to college with her sights set on changing the world.

When talking about issues for girls her age, I hear Sophia repeat the word pressure over and over. It almost sounds like a refrain from an anthem that threatens to define a generation. "There is just, like, a lot of pressure. You feel like you need to be working out, eating healthy all the time, and doing everything you can. I think girls my age feel pressure to eat less and to eat only salads and stuff. I think it all stems from comparing ourselves. Comparing ourselves to each other, our friends, and also models and famous people."

The reality of social comparison for teens is intense. At the adolescent stage of development, the brain and impulses are wired for social connection. Girls this age are constantly assessing their peer groups, how they fit in, and where they stand in relation to others. In the throes of this stage of great identity formation and confusion, girls this age are often constantly comparing themselves to each other and those deemed by society to be "beautiful." They often assess this comparison so effortlessly that going through a day at school can become a running tally of how much she does or doesn't measure up. It becomes instinctual. Like breathing. And much like breathing, it's only with a concentrated effort that they even stop to think about it and actually realize that they are doing it.

For many girls this age, fashion and social media are very much a part of their lives. To meet Sophia in person, you are instantly aware that she has found her own lane in the style department. But she has not arrived there without conflict, keen observation, and questions. While talking about this aspect of her life, she is quick to take direct aim at an industry that sells the idea of a perfect outfit that fits perfectly to a perfect-looking body. "With clothing for example, it seems like there is just one standard body type. There is a brand that is super popular for teenage girls right now that is one-size-fits-all. It's hard because if there is a girl that wants to shop there and she goes in there and things don't fit, she'll think she's fat. It's really bad." When pressed to gauge the actual, translatable size in this "one-size-fits-all" store to other stores that market to teens, Sophia estimates that the only size sold in this highly coveted, popular store would fall in the small to extra-small range. While talking about the absurdity of this, she shares

"There is just, like, a lot of pressure. You feel like you need to be working out, eating healthy all the time, and doing everything you can. I think girls my age feel pressure to eat less and to eat only salads and stuff. I think it all stems from comparing ourselves. Comparing ourselves to each other, our friends, and also models and famous people."

with me further. "The shirts are supposed to be tight-fitting to emphasize a small waist, but the pants are supposed to be wider to emphasize a bigger butt. It's for a very specific body type, and I feel like, right now, those women that everyone feels they are supposed to look like are actually fetishizing cartoon character-like bodies."

Sophia speaks to the evolving and changing expectation and what is appearing to become seemingly the "ideal" body type. She expands on how the proliferation of plastic surgery is becoming more and more extreme. "Everyone is glorifying a certain body type. It's all just so stupid. When I was little and growing up, the ideal body type was just straight skinny. Like the models. Now, it's to have a big butt but no waist. What is the point of putting energy towards that? There is no ideal body. Even mainstream society cannot just pick one body type for a [lengthy] period of time."

Maddeningly—and clearly to the detriment of these young girls—not only are clothing stores promoting a body type that is surgically altered, more developmentally advanced, and generally unrealistic, it is also promoting clothing that is very revealing and sexualized. Emphasizing sex and sexuality for younger girls not only sends a message that more feminine aspects of their anatomy are to be ogled, objectified, and displayed, but also puts them in grave danger for chances of sexual assault and sexual trauma. The seeds that we ultimately would want to take root in our girls about their blossoming sexuality are that it is natural, feminine, and to be revered and celebrated in a healthy way. Instead, those seeds are scattered by cultural and societal winds before they can take root, leading to confusion, shame, and hypersexualized behavior/expression. Girls at younger and younger ages are internalizing a power dark and mysterious that their developing brains can't quite even grasp, and so the message begins to seep in. Sexuality then becomes a weapon that can either be used to their advantage or, with devastating consequences, be used against them.

Sophia confirms that it can be hard to shop at stores marketing to girls her age while still being mindful of showing too much skin. "There are almost fewer options if you are trying to look for something that isn't revealing. People shouldn't feel pressured to dress that way. From every angle you look at it, there's pressure. There is no balance."

Another area of pressure for girls as they traverse the hard-packed trail of adolescence is in trying to piece together who they are and what they are really all about. This all important and identity-forming time of life often comes with forays into different sports, activities and clubs that start to shape and form who our girls start to become. On the one hand, this period is rife with skill building and learning the value of teamwork (while dealing with the ever-present challenges to overcome obstacles that come with participation in an activity or sport). On the other hand, though, and sadly for so many of our girls, these aspects of identity often further drive them into body image concerns and seemingly exacerbate the interconnected and symbiotic relationship between the self and the body. By this stage of life, their physical selves have become so intertwined with every aspect of their being, that what their bodies do becomes inextricably linked to how they look in doing it.

Sophia started doing gymnastics around the age of five. Fully grown at five feet tall, Sophia talks about hearing over the years about being "built like a gymnast." Realizing how her natural genetic build gave her an edge over other teammates gets her emotional and choked up. She reflects now on what it was like to be "glorified" in her sport because of her build, being congratulated for "having a six-pack," and feeling like she was in some ways rewarded for being "one of the smallest on the team." "I think of those girls that weren't the smallest, and the way that they were sometimes treated, and it's such BS. It's almost like a micro-aggression. The coaches aren't bad people, it's just that it's almost like they are sucked into this idea that in order to be a gymnast you need to be tiny and graceful. It's just not true, and it makes me so sad."

Sophia eventually quit gymnastics in high school and admits to struggling with a new way of relating to her body without her identity in the sport. "After I quit, I felt like 'What do I do now?' For ten years, I had coaches telling me what to do about exercise, and I didn't know what to do. I started to feel bad about myself. I had always gotten so much attention for being 'tiny' and having 'a gymnastics body.' " She also admits that, during this tender and confusing time, she began to worry about what people would think of her. "I started to wonder if, without my gymnastics, people would think I had an eating disorder. They are just so common now. When you see someone who is small and tiny, people both praise you but also judge that maybe you have a problem."

As she began to transition out of a life with sports, Sophia began to think about working out and her body in a new way. She had what she describes for herself as a "turning point." "I realized I needed to stop thinking negatively about my body. At school, I work in the multi-needs department with students with disabilities, and I see these kids who are so happy and bright, but they can't do a morning routine by themselves. There are so many places in the world that don't have access to clean water. My body is perfect in the way that it is functioning, and I should be thankful for that. I really had to fix my mindset that my body is perfect just the way that it is, and that it's okay to work out just for health or to be strong, not just to be skinny. I've gained so much confidence now that I have let those feelings go. Now I am proud of myself. It took a while to fix that, but it was so emotional."

Sophia's story is all too common. All over, in homes where moms are paying attention and everything seems "fine," girls are experiencing incredible challenges, threats, and take-downs to their self-esteem and self-worth. Sadly, many girls conceal these struggles, shrug it off as "normal," or overly identify with the cultural or familial norms that reinforce it. For Sophia, confidence and self-image have evolved. She describes herself as having arrived in a better place that seems more firmly rooted on solid ground, although it is, at times, still shaky. She continues to build her strong foundation while peers and friends unfortunately continue to tread water adrift in the sea of negative messages and media influencers.

"If I ever express feeling like I'm not confident with my body, friends will just tell me that I'm skinny and compare themselves to me. People will dismiss me and tell me that I'm 'perfect.' But that's not how I feel, and that doesn't mean anything to me. Some days, I feel gross and different.

I just try to remind myself that I'm lucky to have a body that supports me and can function on my own. There are so many people out there that have disabilities or a variety of different health problems that make every day a lot harder for them. I need to appreciate my body. It's a good thing to want to be healthy and work out, but I want it to be so that I can support my body. I feel like there is pressure to only work out to be skinny. But I remind myself that I am fortunate to have a healthy body, access to health care, and nutrition too. There are so many in the world who are born into places where they can't support their health. No one deserves that, and I try to be aware of that."

Sophia also thinks differently now about what it means to be "beautiful." She admits that, at one time, "beauty" meant having clear skin or looking good in designer jeans. But her perspective has shifted. "Now when I think of beauty, I think about what makes people unique. I just love freckles and different types of birthmarks. There's just something about embracing your body and feeling like it's beautiful." Further, Sophia describes how her ideas of feminine "beauty" have changed in relation to makeup and cosmetics. "It drives me crazy sometimes when girls or celebrities wear tons of makeup and crazy eyeshadow. I feel like it just looks so weird, and I think they look good just the way they are [naturally]. I think highlighting the things that make you different are what make you beautiful."

Sophia is now preparing to head to college, with dreams and visions of impacting the world. As an active volunteer for people with special needs and a budding activist, her sharp intellect primes her for making her mark. Her ability to succeed in these endeavors will depend on her ability to see herself as powerful and capable of rocking boats, making changes, and using her voice. Her empowered sense of self—rather than a diminished, tentative sense of worth and value—will inevitably pave her way.

"I think it's important to be aware of other people in the world. I am aware of how fortunate I am, and [I'm aware] of those who are neglected by society. It's important to have empathy for others, be grateful for what you have, and use what you have to help others. When I think of body image, I think we need to stop dwelling on being upset about our bodies. What is the point of getting so wrapped up in negativity about my body when there are so many other things going on in the world? There are certain things that need to be put first. Human rights need to be put first."

REFLECTION TIME

What do you think of when you reflect on your own adolescence? Were there strong messages that impacted the way you feel about your body then? Do those issues still impact you now?

Think about your current age demographic. What are the messages that you see from advertisers in regards to clothing, appearance, and pressures? How do you feel about it?

Sophia leaned into her values in order to move beyond cultural pressures about her weight, shape, and appearance. What values are most meaningful for you now? How can you remind yourself of those values if you struggle with a negative day about your body, weight, age, shape, or appearance?

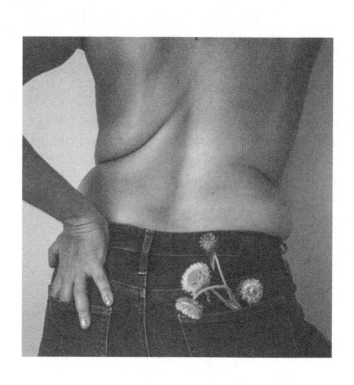

4

GOOD OR BAD

"Our Relationship to Food"

"Are you here to lose weight or to gain weight?!"

─────────────────────

That was the question that the Jenny Craig© consultant asked me the first time we met sometime around 1990. The idea to go on a diet had been mine, in spite of being at a "normal" weight for my height and my age. When my new diet coach asked me that question, I was truly baffled. Wasn't she seeing what I was seeing? Clearly, I needed to lose weight. But the question suggested that she wasn't sure. Still, she took my money, and signed me, at the age of fifteen, up for the program that was populated almost entirely by middle-aged women, thus ushering me into a club whose membership, it would seem, was for life.

The diet industry. The billions of dollars generated by the diet industry. Have you ever stopped and thought for a moment about what it would mean if every woman on the planet woke up and decided to never diet again? Do you have any idea of the sheer amount of lost revenue that would ensue? The dieting business is serious business. And as I have experienced firsthand, it is always more than willing to take your money, no matter what it will ultimately cost you.

Unlike a lot of issues in the world, the diet industry does not discriminate. If they will gladly enroll a fifteen-year-old girl with a smile as they take a payment . . . and they will enroll every other age and gender. "Dieting" is ageless and genderless and can be a lifetime carousel. For Ansara, who is twenty-seven years old, her dieting experience began in college. "In college, I tried different diets. I tried vegan; I tried vegan keto; but it was really unhealthy and not sustainable long term. I tried a lot of different diets while working out intensely. It was so unhealthy and wasn't doing my body any good. It was always really restrictive. I felt like I was reaping the benefits of losing weight, but that ultimately wasn't really doing me any good either. The messages of dieting are that you have to do the extreme and that if you don't, then you are failing. I made a conscious decision to diet, but I hate seeing how easy it is to fall into that trap."

The trap that is dieting. I have lived long enough now to have seen—and participated in—several dieting trends over the decades. Many of them are contradictory. Many of them are based on questionable "science." All of them are restrictive in some way. Most are generally unsustainable on many levels. Keto, paleo, no-carb, low-carb, intermittent fasting, juicing, cleansing. Honestly: It's exhausting. It's confusing. It's constantly changing. And while the fads come and go, one constant is that most diets are almost always abandoned, only to result in shame, frustration, and an increased likelihood of developing a bingeing problem. Data on dieting also shows that fad and intense diets most often result in the weight lost plus more being gained again in short order.

First, before the chorus reaches fever pitch about how "unhealthy and obese" Americans are, let me be clear. I am well aware that the Standard American Western Diet, with its fast

food—heavily processed and high in sugar content—is not only not health promoting but also disease promoting. I do not now, nor will I ever, endorse a diet consisting of an excessive amount of highly processed foods, fast foods, foods high in sugar, and lacking in plants and other vital foods.

Second, let me also be clear about another point that I think drives the diet industry: I believe, without a doubt, that weight bias is alive and well in both society and the medical community, and that the idea of health at every size needs to be encouraged and embraced.

Common beliefs about "health" have been hijacked by the diet and fitness industry (even the medical community), and they often insinuate that "thinness and weight loss always equals better health." Losing weight has become some kind of "health holy grail," in spite of the fact that weight loss can sometimes be the result of an overly restrictive diet, overexercising, or a veiled eating disorder or body image disturbance. YouTube, Instagram, TikTok, magazines, and blogs are all chock full of an endless array of "influencers and gurus" promoting disordered and distorted thinking and behaviors under the guise of health and fitness. In addition, sometimes weight loss can indicate the presence of disease rather than its absence. Crohn's disease, celiac disease, cancer, and anorexia nervosa are just a few dangerous and deadly medical conditions characterized by rapid weight loss and marked thinness. Over the years, I have collected many stories of individuals being praised for weight loss when their body was actually being ravaged by disease. They often hear, "You look great!" when the true story was that they didn't feel great at all.

"I feel like the media is starting to embrace the variety in shape, but still the weight aspect seems to be an issue," shared Renee, age thirty-four. "There is just so much pressure to lose weight to be 'healthy.' I think that there needs to be a variety in what we see as healthy in terms of weight."

Weight bias is alive and well in the medical community. Over the years, many of my clients with an eating disorder have heard firsthand from their pediatricians or primary care doctors about the need to lose weight, despite being young, going through puberty or hormonal changes, or having no identified medical problem or risk factor. This recommendation is often made purely by looking at the scale or the BMI. The Body Mass Index, in spite of the fact that it is outdated (it was developed in 1830), is not a consistent or solid metric for health, was only developed for middle-aged men, and yet it continues to be a standard tool used within the medical community. Lisa Carroll, RD, MS, LPN, is a dietitian that specializes in weight management, eating disorders, and binge eating. Lisa sounds off about the dangers of using the BMI to determine one's health. "The BMI is pretty archaic. I use that word specifically because it was developed a long time ago, before there were calculators and computers. It was a simple equation that was easy to compute. Unfortunately, our society has stuck with that and hasn't really progressed."

Alyssa was eight years old when her pediatrician sounded the alarm about her weight. By the time she was age eleven, she was hearing both from her doctor and then her parents a strong message about her body. In spite of the fact that she was an active girl, involved in school sports, and tall for her age, that message was, "Something is wrong with your body. It's your fault. It's up to you to fix it." Alyssa continued to struggle with her body all throughout middle school and high school. Her self-esteem became embedded with her weight. Her confidence bottomed out. By the time she was finishing high school, Alyssa was an athlete, a straight-A student, and was headed to a top-notch college, where she would become an elite athlete in her sport—all the while feeling "fat," "unlovable," and "not good enough."

While in college and preparing to pursue a path to the Olympics, she rapidly gained a significant amount of weight even with her dedicated training and a lack of significant change in lifestyle habits. She began to suspect an underlying medical issue, but still, her doctors still sent the same message. "Something is wrong with your body. It's your fault. It's up to you to fix it." It took well over a year to accurately diagnose her with polycystic ovarian syndrome, a chronic illness resulting in insulin resistance, which, at that point, she had been suffering with for years. By the time her doctor made the diagnosis, her hopes and dreams of the Olympics were gone.

"Sometimes when you are focused on what you're eating, calories, and your weight, you forget to think about who you are and your true purpose. Thinking about myself as a whole person helps me to stay on the right path."

— BECKY, 19

She was suffering from anxiety and depression; and her self-worth, due to the message that her body image issues were the direct result of her lack of self-control and behavioral choices, were in serious need of an overhaul.

Meredith, forty-eight years old, also suffered a misdiagnosis that doctors initially deemed a self-control and weight loss issue. At age fourteen, she noticed that she was having weakness in her calves. Over the years, Meredith continued to hear from doctors that her medical problems were about her weight, and that weight loss was the answer. It wasn't until she was thirty-one years old that she was accurately diagnosed with muscular dystrophy. Now wheelchair bound, Meredith's message to girls and women is to trust themselves and their bodies, and to not give in to weight bias as an explanation for potential medical issues: " 'Fat' doesn't always equal 'bad or unhealthy.' I think that so much focus is put on 'fat.' You can eat well and work out and still some doctor's scale puts you in a category on the BMI that puts you in that 'obese' category. And I feel like there are a lot of people who feel like being 'fat' is the worst thing that you could be. I would tell people to just listen to your body. If your doctor tells you that something that is wrong with your body is about your weight, push back. Even when I was fourteen, I felt like I knew that something else was wrong."

Meredith is working hard now to come to terms with her body, its limitations, and her relationship to herself. "What I say from time to time is that 'my body is full of so much betrayal that it could be an episode of Dynasty!' I have made peace with a lot of it, and there are still obviously things that I wish I could do. I've been mad. I get sad, but I don't get angry every day. I can't focus on that. It's there. Lately, I have been making myself just sit and look in the mirror and just say, 'This is you.' I'm not ashamed of it, but I've been grappling with it. I just sit and look at it and say, 'Every part of this is me.' And every part of it is frustrating and beautiful and everything all at the same time. And I just allow myself to feel all of that. Sometimes, too, it's the wheelchair itself. Sometimes I would like to just look in the mirror and not see the chair."

For so many girls and women, their identity becomes entwined with their bodies and their weight. Girls and women start to shape core beliefs about who they are and what they are or aren't capable of based on what they see in the mirror and what they see on the scale. Society echoes these messages, and girls and women begin to dig quite a hole in their own sense of self-worth. Peers, parents, and even doctors can also be influenced by weight bias and diet culture. Unfortunately, sometimes they in turn, contribute negatively to our self-worth by unknowingly making comments that also dig deep into body image issues.

"I want people to stop judging those of us who are considered 'fat' based on how we look and judge us by what we do and what we bring to the community." At fifty-six years old, Mary Beth knows she is a valuable person to the community and to her family even though she is judged first by her size. "I know that I matter. I know that I make a difference. It's one of the things I want to do, to leave this place better than when I arrived. I feel like people who are considered 'fat' are not taken seriously, because of the fact that people look at us and just say, 'You're overweight. You're fat.' As a plus-sized woman going out into the world every day, you can't just throw on sweats and pull your hair back into a ponytail. Because we know that we are going to get judged by that: 'They've really let themselves go.' Whereas if a size two woman did that, others would say, 'Oh, how cute. She's so fresh-faced and confident.' We feel like we have to go that extra mile to make sure that our hair and makeup and nails are done, so that if we are in the community, people will not automatically judge us."

As a nation, we are obsessed with diet culture. And yet we are simultaneously suffering with incredibly high rates of health issues. While the rates of diseases like autoimmune, cancer, and heart disease skyrocket, we seem to be becoming more and more confused and muddled about food and our bodies. In terms of disease prevention and longevity, there is no question that there is a mountain of scientific evidence to support that food is our frontline defense against illness and that what we choose to eat absolutely impacts our physical health, our gut microbiome, and our mental health. The problem with diet culture is the rampant misinformation, the rigidity it requires, the lack of common sense, the unsustainability long term, the immense pressure that it puts on weight as the most important metric, and the incredible amount of self-judgment that results in thinking about food and weight.

Are there individuals that need to consult with their doctor about how their weight is impacting their health? Absolutely. But there is a difference between weight loss for disease prevention or disease management versus wanting or needing to be thinner to feel a sense of self-worth. In instances where weight loss is essential to health and vitality, it's important to fully understand the mindset required for lasting and positive results, which is not often the mindset that comes from following a fad or extreme diet.

Lisa Carroll believes that rather than helping us become healthier as a population, diet culture is creating many problems for many people. "When it comes down to diets in general, research has not shown that any one diet is the most effective. We don't have evidence to say, for example, something like 'low carb diets across the board will work for 80 percent of individuals.' What it is saying, basically, is that if someone is looking for a means to lose weight and keep the weight off, which is the most important aspect, there is no one diet that is going to be the most effective. Because of the increased information on social media and in our culture about diets, people begin to assume that what works for one will work for all, and it's a bit of a square-peg-in-a-round-hole situation." Lisa believes that all the focus on dieting and "clean eating" creates an atmosphere where people get stuck thinking about thinking about food in all-or-nothing categories, like "good" and "bad."

Lisa adds, "I think all foods can fit. Instead of thinking about food as 'good food' and 'bad food,' I talk to people about their behaviors. It gets really confusing [for them] because people adopt all kinds of rules that don't really apply to their bodies and preferences, and then they don't stick to them, because it's too restrictive or doesn't include things that they really enjoy. If people can be more proficient in the array of eating that life encompasses, like going to a party or a restaurant, you can really broaden your horizon and know and manage better what works for you."

"I don't feel like I have to go on a diet or anything. I feel like my body weight is just fine the way that it is. If I am at the pool or something, and if I'm wearing a bikini, I sometimes feel like my stomach is too big and I feel like I need to be able to change that. But now that I'm looking back on that, I feel like maybe I don't want to change that. I don't want to be someone who is always trying to perfect who they are."

— SCARLETT, 11

Lisa acknowledges that body image and the psychological drive for thinness is a huge issue in the work that she does as a dietician. "Often, people come to me with a number they want to be on the scale. They pick a number that they think is going to make them happy and make them healthy. I try to steer them away from that number and instead get back to basics. We start to take out some of the problematic behaviors, like restricting carbs all day and then bingeing on them at night, or not taking the time to slow down and eat, and then, overeating quickly. It's also important to look at not only behaviors with food and exercise, but also mental and emotional wellness. I ask people, 'Are you getting enough sleep? Are you getting enough hydration? Are you practicing healthy forms of self-care?' Once we begin to clear all of that up, their weight starts to fall in the range of where it should be. That might be the number that they were reaching for, and it might not be. For some people, that might be a higher weight status, due to genetics and body type. So, even if technically they could be healthy to be at a lower weight, their body is going to fight it, because of this idea of 'set point.' And there has to be a bit of acceptance of that disappointment."

In talking about how to walk away from diet culture and make strides based on overall improvements in health, Lisa says, "I think it is important for people to shift their mindset away from diet culture, which is focused on what people 'shouldn't do': 'I shouldn't eat that' . . . 'I shouldn't do that' . . . 'I can't have this or that.' I want people to think instead about what they 'could be doing': 'I could be taking time to get enough sleep. I could be taking time to go to the grocery store. I could be taking time out of a busy week to do some food prep. I could keep a water bottle with me during the day. I could find a way to move my body in a way that I like consistently that is sustainable.' That shift helps people move away from the shame piece and the trap that is 'good girl' or 'bad girl.' " When asked about her personal relationship to food as a dietitian that promotes not only wellness but also balance, Lisa is quick to share a few of her favorite foods; "My go-to is any creamy dip. A crunch and a dip—I'll never say no to that. And, of course, chocolate! A warm brownie is my love language. . . that, and sour cream."

Diet culture has undoubtedly shaped our language and our shared beliefs. Ask a little girl what foods are 'good,' and she is likely to say something like 'cupcakes' or maybe 'pizza.' Ask most girls around eleven or twelve years old or women who are older which foods are 'good,' and she is likely to tell you 'carrots' or 'salad.' Of course, carrots and salad are health-promoting and nutritious. The problem of thinking about food this way is that it creates this belief that some foods are 'good' and some foods are 'bad' and that eating foods that fall into those categories can subsequently tell us whether or not we are 'good' or 'bad.'

Another part of this trap of 'good and bad' when it comes to the diet industry is the daily dance that so many girls and women do with their bathroom scale.

Ugh, the scale. Can we talk about our obsession with the scale? Have you ever seen the inside of one?

I have.

I have seen girls and women take a hammer to this piece of plastic, this beacon of their worth and value, only to reveal that its secret, magical inner workings are actually just a few pieces of metal and a tiny spring. This beast with the ability to determine whether or not the day will be a 'good one' or a 'bad one' and decides whether or not someone needs to eat only 'good food' or can indulge in some 'bad food': its innards expose something so simple and yet so powerful. The women I have seen who are courageous enough to listen to and trust their bodies instead and to destroy or throw out their scale are angry. Very, very angry. At the way that scale has made them feel about themselves. At the way that scale has driven them to behave. At the sheer force of power that had been handed over to that little thing on the floor in their bathroom. Day after day after day.

Kimberly, twenty-seven years old, says that, growing up, she didn't have a strong foundation about nutrition in her life. She remembers drinking an energy drink in sixth grade and eating a diet that often-included chips, soda and sugar. She remembers starting the day in high school with Pop-Tarts® or breakfast sandwiches from fast-food restaurants, and then would often not eat lunch. Over time, she began to learn more about nutrition, initially through her high school lacrosse coaches, while also developing a pattern of excessive exercise to deal with what she felt was unwanted weight gain. She says that around this time in her life that she felt like she was 'constantly working out.'

In college, Kimberly was still struggling to eat a balanced diet and began to fall into different fads that she had learned about on social media, one of which encouraged what she now describes as a "toxic cycle" of "before-and-after" photos between workouts and long periods of fasting. By sophomore year in college, despite feeling "strong and confident" because of her intense workout regime, her weight was at its heaviest. "The number on the scale really began to mess with me," she shared. She also reported feeling highly triggered by the photos she was taking or seeing in social media, and she decided to try a keto or low-carb diet. While her weight goals seemed to be moving in the direction that she desired, she says that she began to notice decreased energy for running and her overall fitness performance started to lag, forcing her to ultimately revert to walking instead of running. Her obsession with the scale began in earnest, to the point of even restricting water intake so as to see the result on the scale. She remembers running races and would bypass water stations on the course, also being sure to not drink water after the race until she got home and weighed herself first. "To me it was worth it to see a pound decrease on the scale, even though my body needed the hydration."

Looking back on it now, she says, "It was all really unhealthy. There was a time when I was very fit, but I wasn't happy with my body. I was running a lot of miles and doing well in races, but I couldn't enjoy it, because my thighs touched. I got so fixated on these minor details that other people probably didn't notice. But I did."

Kimberly says that, over time, she began to shift away from thinking about food, weight and her body in this way. "Now I don't weigh myself nearly as often. I will weigh myself once a week, as a check in, but it doesn't affect me. Before, if I would have gained five pounds, I would have been very uncomfortable in my skin, and it would destroy the rest of my day thinking about it.

Now I am okay with whatever the number is. I feel strong. I take care of my body. I feel great in my skin. I have so many other things in my life that I am proud of. The way that I look is very minor in my everyday life now. My body has developed. It's going to change. That is okay, and I honestly love my body."

Dieting. Thinking about food. Counting calories. Getting on and off the scale every day. Feeling good. Feeling bad. It's all so consuming. And it's also seductive. Seductive in the fact that engaging in these behaviors can often give someone a sense that they have control of their life, at least when it comes to their size and shape. Life, as we all know, is rife with problems, some of them quite challenging to solve. Family issues, financial issues, relationships, trauma. The promise of dieting is that it drives a false sense of control. We may, often unknowingly, feel helpless in areas of our lives where we can't find a solution or want to deny what is really going on. Identifying our bodies as "the problem" so often distracts from bigger, more pressing, and far more real problems. And the diet industry is far too happy to convince us that they have the solution to our "problem."

The conversations around health and wellness needs to shift away from dieting. Dieting can lead to obsession, low self-esteem, and feelings of poor self-worth. Dieting can eat up precious bandwidth in our resources for time and energy that, quite frankly, girls and women could better put to use elsewhere. The world needs fewer women obsessing over counting calories and more women instead obsessing over how to best use their gifts in this world that so desperately needs the generous sharing of them.

So, what's the alternative to dieting? How do we find this elusive balance? Kimberly believes that it is possible. "The balance of being healthy and feeding your body what it wants and needs is not impossible. It's actually ten times easier than dieting. Dieting can so often lead to binge-ing. I can and want to enjoy all foods in life. When I feel restricted, that can feed into depression. That's what feeds into body dysmorphia. Suddenly, food isn't this thing that can nourish you, it feels like it's your enemy. It's such an unhealthy relationship, and diet culture feeds into that.

Food should be your friend. Food should never be your enemy. It took me a long time to look at different types of food and to say, 'I don't hate any of you, I love all of you, I just love this more than I love that. I love carrots, but I hate celery.' It's finding balance. It's tough though, because it's not [about finding balance] in our society, and I don't see it being that way for a very long time."

Sadly, I agree with Kimberly that it seems that dieting is here to stay: It's far too profitable. It's far too trendy. But I also have hope. I have hope because I feel like many girls and women are slowly coming to the realization that weight-focused diets don't serve them well. Many of them are coming to the conclusion that extreme dieting takes commitment, action, and planning, and yet, it most often results in less energy as well as feelings of failure, guilt, and shame. It's not sustainable.

Those that are letting go of dieting behaviors and pressures about weight are slowly realizing that healthy lifestyle choices also take commitment, action, and planning. But they, instead of depleting, most often result in more energy, better health outcomes, and longevity. And these choices can certainly last a lifetime.

Same effort. Different mindset. Polar opposite outcomes.

Having been a dieter in my past, I have come to embrace the reality that life with food is messy and imperfect. So are our bodies. So are our lives in general. It's about balance, letting go of perfection, and finding the joy in all types of foods. I made a choice long ago that nourishing our bodies is for wellness and that it's also important to allow for food to be a part of life's pleasures and gatherings. It's about trusting our bodies, letting go of shame, and creating new narratives.

Olivia, twelve years old, is a soccer player and a runner. In addition to sports or hanging out with her dog and her friends, she loves taking trips with her family. She shares how parts of those memories have been shaped by finding fun spots to eat along the way. "Almost every vacation we go on, we find a donut shop and we all try new donuts that we haven't had before. My favorite was Pink Box Donuts in Las Vegas. Some flavors are really random. Once I got this poop emoji donut. It was two donuts stacked up!"

Life is long if we eat lots of plants and take good care of our bodies with food. But life is also too short not to eat a donut every once in a while.

Let's ditch the diets!

LET'S TALK!

Stop labeling foods as "good" or "bad." Also watch labeling food as "junk food." Instead, use categories such as "likes" and "dislikes" or "preferences."

Talk about food based on facts, not judgments. For example, foods that come in packages as opposed to fresh foods.

Find foods that you enjoy from all food groups. Stop vilifying entire food groups such as "carbs," "fats," or whatever the diet trend of the day deems as "bad for you."

Be mindful of balance. Choose plenty of high-quality, health-promoting foods and allow for fun, convenience, and pleasure at times.

Make a vow to stop extreme diets.

Throw away your scale. Let your body guide you by how your clothing fits. Don't let the scale determine your worth, your value, or what kind of day that you are having.

Be willing to honestly look at your own potential weight bias.

Don't let false metrics such as weight or BMI determine your sense of health and wellness.

Talk to your doctor about your risk factors, get routine checkups, and set goals around your lifestyle habits and behaviors.

"I do worry about dieting. Most of my friends are shorter than me, so I know that I should weigh more than them. But they weigh less than me, and I don't like weighing more than them."

— STELLA, 9

5

BEGINNER'S LANE

"Fitness and Exercise Culture"

"If you are in Beginner Class today and you need some time to just get comfortable with yourself physically, that's okay. You can be here as long as you need."[4]

It's 8:45 a.m., and I have just finished a workout that I streamed from my iPad in the basement, followed by a "weekly talk" with the fitness guru whose method I was practicing. It's a Monday morning, and I didn't complete the workout because I had been "bad" the previous weekend. I didn't work out to "undo" anything that I had eaten the day before. I worked out because when I do, the breath that I exhale literally breathes energy into my day. It's become a way to access something within so that I can sustain the day ahead. Whether that's being a mom, doing my job as a photographer, or going to my clinical therapy practice, getting the blood pumping pumps me up to face it all head on and be focused and alert. So, most Monday mornings, with a full schedule and long to-do list, I fire up a workout to get fired up. Exercise has become such a holy part of my routine, and I am clear on the positive and self-respecting reasons why. That, however, hasn't always been the case.

I've tried almost every sport imaginable as a kid growing up; I was never really an athlete. I am not someone who thrives on competition. The truth is that most of my life with exercise was about caloric burn. For a long time, exercise was about changing, shaping, and controlling my body—how it looked, what it weighed. There were days after school in high school that friends would make plans to hang out. I often skipped out on those plans, to go on to the gym to do a workout, only stopping after I hit a certain number of calories burned on the machine's digital display. In college, I decided to become a "runner." It definitely was not because I loved or even liked running. In fact, I hated running. But I told myself that it was the best way to torch calories; and so, I logged mile after mile in an attempt to sculpt my body into something that I thought it should be. After graduate school and right before my wedding, I clocked hours in the gym in preparation for my wedding day. I was, after all, going to wear a strapless and form-fitting gown. Later, I found myself exercising during pregnancy, so as not to "gain too much weight," so that my body could "bounce back." Then, I had to dig deep to find the energy to exercise no matter how badly I needed sleep when my son was born. I wanted to fit into my pre-pregnancy clothing. On and on it went. The idea that fitness was always about burning energy rather than generating it was underpinning a lot of my exercise habits for a lot of years.

Over time, however, I began to see the importance of being grateful for what my body could do. I began to see the importance of giving my body rest, of listening, of taking time off when I had an injury, and of seriously rethinking my entire "why" with exercise. Learning to accept, honor, and listen to my body, even if it meant being a "beginner" again at forty-four years old in a new fitness class, was ultimately more health-promoting and positive than beating my body into submission with a grueling workout.

"Stay in the beginner lane as long as you need." The fitness professional who spoke these words to me on that Monday morning through the Internet is adamant that, regardless of her

massive celebrity following, the goal is not to look like someone else. Her reminder that "self-love is a lot more effective when it comes to your health" is like a breath of fresh air. She also speaks regularly about fitness incorporating principles of "balance, spirit, soul, energy, and wholeness." This is different than the message that you are likely to hear in many gyms, programs, or fitness centers. Typically, you hear things like "pain is weakness leaving the body," "no pain, no gain," or "push through the pain."[4]

A lot of fitness professionals subscribe to the idea that you can radically and quickly change the shape of your body—complete and utter transformation—if you just commit to it enough and work hard enough. The health and fitness industry is a powerful and hungry beast, and the spoils often go to those who are the most restrictive, weigh the least, and work out the most. Sure, there are some voices that speak to balance and moderation in exercise. They just aren't particularly loud, and they certainly don't dominate the conversation. The fitness industry often offers up a one-size-fits-all approach, and that is generally to attain the smallest size, the most muscularly defined, or the leanest body that you can inhabit, even though it requires overexercising, undereating and sometimes engaging in downright dangerous behavior to burn calories from our bodies is anything but health-promoting.

In my early forties, a friend convinced me to try her morning workout class. I entered the gym, was asked no questions about my fitness level or my health, did not warm up or cool down, and was put through the paces of an incredibly intense workout. I left there feeling unwell and was sore for days in a way that did not feel good to me. Something about it felt dangerous and irresponsible, not just on the part of the gym owner, but also for my own well-being.

Allie, at twenty-eight years old, is starting her own business as a certified personal trainer and health and wellness coach. Allie says that she believes that the fitness industry is "in transition." "One of the things I was introduced to first in this industry is different measurements of value. Whether it was a measurement of value based on how you look, or how much weight you can lift, or a combination of both. If you weren't working for one, you were working for the other. That's what you were going into the gym to do. It felt very black or white. You were either succeeding or failing. The more I was exposed to that, the more I was feeling how toxic that was. I was wondering why I was doing all of these things that were supposed to be so good for me but were feeling so miserable. I felt like, 'This can't actually be good. What's happening? What's going on?' "

During elementary school, Allie says she developed "very disordered behaviors around eating." What started as a way of coping and creating "a safe environment" for herself with food had become by high school a "chronic and severe issue." As she further shares, "There were things going on in my life, and I felt so out of control. I was answering to other people, couldn't make choices of my own, and there was this little pocket of my life that felt like 'mine.' It felt like I could control something. So, I restricted my food intake all day and then I would binge. It felt secret and private. That led to me gaining a lot of weight, and because of my age and expectations around me, it was immediately pointed out to me. I was a competitive figure skater, and when I look back on it now, I wasn't overweight at all. But I was being compared to girls who were older and in a different developmental stage, and I felt incredibly defeated. I felt like I was not good enough, and I was constantly striving for something and never felt content."

Allie says that over time, these patterns led her to a place where she was deemed "morbidly obese" by the time she was sixteen years old. In addition to starting to have health issues, Allie says, "That the weight gain really messed up my body image. I was called names like 'tire belly' or 'fat pig.' I got really depressed."

After a while, Allie was finally able to open up to her mom and asked for help. At that time, treatment included medication, seeing a physician specialist, going to group therapy, and hospitalizations to help with her mood disorder. She also found fitness and began to work with a personal trainer.

"I started to have moments where I realized that I was doing things that I thought I would never be able to do. I started to see that I could remove this ceiling that I had set and try not to identify with the limitations." While positive shifts were happening for Allie, there was also a

"I feel like knowing and seeing what my body is capable of motivates me and encourages me— I am working hard for something. To be able to see the goal pay off, that is so much more worthwhile than staring at the mirror and feeling like my body is thin. As an athlete, I don't want that, because I can instead do what I want my body to do."

— RILEY, 15

dark side to her lifestyle with fitness. "Once I got my bearings in the gym, the rigidity came. I started working with a coach, and it became about 'What are your goals now? How much weight do you want to lose? How much body fat do you want to have? How much weight do you want to lift?' It was all about these measurements. The predominant message was 'We are not going to stop until we get to that goal.' " In order to achieve those goals, Allie began a series of daily behaviors and rituals that quickly became quite intense. "I was working out, tracking my macros, and felt a lot of pressure to keep it up. I got to a point where I was using a food scale and scooping off the top if I was one gram off. I weighed myself two to three times a day. I was so deprived. I wasn't even eating real food. I was constantly feeling starved, because I was mostly having supplements and not eating enough actual food. My body was actually starving."

While Allie started slowly realizing that what she was doing didn't feel good, the messages that she got about her body were at first reinforcing the behaviors. "I was hearing feedback like, 'You are killing it,' 'You look amazing,' 'You look like a totally different person,' and 'I've never seen you look so healthy.' I believed all of that for a while, but then I realized that, while everyone was telling me that, I was constantly thinking things like, 'I don't feel healthy at all. How is this healthy? I feel like garbage. My body hurts all the time. All I want to do is sleep and eat. My body is so, so hungry.' "

Allie says there was a moment where she felt a complete state of exhaustion, and she says she "just broke": "I looked in the mirror one day and felt like, 'I don't think this is what I wanted. I thought I did for a really long time, but this body doesn't feel good to me. Yeah, I look really strong, and you can see these well-defined muscles, but why did I do this? Why am I waking up at five in the morning to do this?' I was so stressed and anxious. To be that fit felt like a full-time job. I got to this point where I realized that it had totally gotten ahead of me and had stolen all of my freedom. I found myself in extreme adrenal fatigue. I was relying on caffeine to keep going, because my body was in a constant state of stress and I was overtraining my brains out. I wasn't giving myself enough recovery time. I wasn't getting enough sleep. I was wrecking myself."

The turning point for Allie, ironically enough, was in diving deeper into fitness and wellness to find her way out. "I began to talk to other trainers and professionals who helped me shift and see things in a different way. I found a trainer who would keep it so simple. If I was complaining of being tired, she would tell me, 'Sleep.' If I was hungry, she would tell me, 'Go have a snack.' It was like getting permission to be intuitive and listen to my body again. And it seemed revolutionary. The shift in body image for me started to happen when I started to realize that my body was more than something to look at. It started to become about what my body was doing. I still have days where I wake up and I look in the mirror and see myself the way I did in high school when my body was really different. I have to acknowledge that a lot of that isn't coming from how my body really looks, it's coming from other things, and it's just manifesting itself in the way that I am looking at my body."

Now Allie is putting herself at the forefront of a new wave within the fitness industry. "I have intentionally placed myself more in the space of wellness. That's where I feel good supporting people. I want to promote a more holistic approach. I don't want to participate in this black-and-white environment where achieving certain goals equals value." How has Allie's body image changed as a result of her experiences in fitness? "For so long, my body image was through the lens of what makes everyone else comfortable, which in our society is entirely dictated by things that we see online or in movies or in shows. All of that is edited, perfected, and literally designed. Even the people who we are seeing in these ads or movies don't look like that. And they know that they don't look like that. Everything I do for my body now is so that I can have these experiences that I want to have. If I want to go rock climbing, or on a hike, or on a walk with a friend—I need my body to take me there and take me through that. My body is ultimately the way to express myself. The way I dress. The way that I present myself with body language. It's all pieces of me that I want to present to the world."

It's not just the fitness industry that needs a bit of an adjustment in perspective when it comes to women and their bodies. The field of athletics often buys into this idea as well that athleticism and one's overall physique go hand in hand. Many sports and teams today still focus on weight, shape, and appearance, sometimes requiring measurements or weight checks. Elena, twenty-eight years old and a former collegiate rower, reports feeling confused about her body in college. She knew that she was the fastest rower on the team, but because of required team weigh-ins, she also knew that she was the heaviest, outweighing her fellow teammates by almost forty pounds. Instead of feeling proud about her accomplishment as the fastest and the strongest, she focused instead on the weight and felt that her body had failed her. She doubted herself and her abilities, frequently asking herself, "How can I be an elite athlete if I'm this heavy?"

Many who engage in athletics have highly competitive, driven, and hard-working personalities. On the track or the court, that's great. But when the goal becomes about what they see in the mirror or on the scale, those attributes can often backfire. Reese, age fifteen, runs track and cross country. She talks openly about the conversations that she and fellow teammates have about their bodies and the comparison. "Being on the cross-country team, I think about myself as heavier. I am a size two, and I'm super small, but some of my closest friends are size double zero, and that has become the norm for me. So, when I stand next to them, I think of myself as heavy-set. It isn't a bad thing, but sometimes I think, 'Wow, I'm big.'" What we long have thought of as "locker-room talk" for boys, assessing and evaluating girls' bodies, it turns out, is also "locker-room talk" for the girls. And it's not just the culture of runners. Other sports whose cultures often—whether knowingly or unknowingly—promote body image disturbance and pressure for thinness include gymnastics, dance, figure skating, swimming, sports with competitive weight requirements, and more.

While the field of sports, athletics, and fitness culture can sometimes have a negative impact on girls and women and their body image, there is also an incredible opportunity for sports and athletics to develop a sense of strength and pride in their physical abilities.

Aimee, twenty-two years old, was born with tibial hemimelia, a congenital condition whereby her tibia bones did not develop in utero. Aimee underwent a double amputation when she was

"Growing up, I always felt fairly confident, but I also felt too skinny and awkward. I remember when, in seventh grade, a coach told me that I was part of 'the Ethiopian clan,' referring to me and a few other girls in my class who were skinny and late to mature. Now I recognize how inappropriate it was for an adult woman to make that statement and that she was, perhaps, uncomfortable with her own body. I was embarrassed that my body wasn't as "womanly" as some of my friends' bodies. I felt a little bit like a 'freak' when I was so late going through puberty in high school."

— CAMILLE, 44

just six months old. Since then, Aimee's life has been an interlude of surgeries, prosthetic fittings, new pairs of legs, physical therapy, and, above all, finding ways to "blend in"—even with how different her life looks than most other girls her age.

Sports for Aimee became a way to blossom, to see herself and her life in a whole new way. In her freshman year of high school, she decided to join the diving team. She has always loved the water but didn't think that she could be on the swim team, because she didn't think that she could make the times that the other, "able-bodied" swimmers were doing. During her sophomore year, her diving coach told her that athletes with disabilities were in a different time category than the able-bodied swimmers. He challenged her to get in the pool to do a fifty-yard freestyle. Fearing that it wouldn't be "good enough" but being well-versed in facing her fears, she decided to get in the pool to "see how it goes." When she was finished, her time was less than half of what the other swimmers in her category were swimming. Having glimpsed a new reality of her physical potential, she joined the swim team and then went on to place second that year in the state tournament for the 150-yard freestyle. By her senior year of high school, she placed first in all four events, making her the only woman on her team to go to the state championship three years in a row, an accomplishment that she says made her feel "over the moon." Today, Aimee still holds the state record for the 100-yard breaststroke.

Now, as a college graduate, she is learning what else she is capable of; yet, at the same time, navigating a new reality with her body and body image. "I still swim recreationally. But since I have stopped swimming and being coached through workouts and keeping my body fit, I lost a lot of weight after high school. I had to figure out how I wanted my body to look because I needed new prosthetic legs and a complete socket change. I had to figure out how to work out and how I could eat right and still be comfortable in my prosthetics and my skin. Everyone wants to be skinny and with a big butt, but I can't do squats. That has been tricky to figure out: how I want my body to look and how I can get there."

As a former athlete studying now to be an esthetician, Aimee talks about trying to figure out who she is and who she wants to be. "I have big dreams. I struggle with the day-to-day decisions of how to make that happen. It's a process. I feel like I am in that stage right now." When asked about wanting to go into the beauty industry, with its high standards and messages for women, Aimee is on a mission to get the balance right. "Knowing what compliments your body type, your skin type, your hair color, or your eye color can make you feel more confident. I think that confidence is worn on the outside. I think that confidence makes a woman beautiful." When asked if she feels like she is beautiful, Aimee responds, softly but firmly, "I do feel like I am beautiful. Yeah. I'll leave it at that."

Aimee is such a great example of how sports, exercise, and movement can foster gratitude, skill building, and empowerment for girls and women. Yes, we do see an overarching emphasis on how the body looks in sports and fitness, but the truth is that engaging in athletics and exercise can serve as a positive outlet for a lot of girls and women. For a lot of young girls, looking up to female athletes offers a counterpoint to a toxic celebrity culture and showcases the potential and power of the female form. There are a ton of stories of women feeling more empowered because of being part of a team or participating in a sport. And it's exciting to see young girls embracing the power and aptitude of their physical selves through sports by emulating women like Abby Wambach, Serena Williams, or Ronda Rousey. These role models, voices, and women speaking out about health at every size and weight are out there. You just have to go looking for them. And they can be amazing forces to counteract the negative messages that girls and women can internalize about sports, exercise, and movement.

At the end of the day, our relationship to exercise, sports, and fitness is an extension of our relationships to ourselves. It offers us the opportunity to practice self-love over self-judgment. It offers us the ability to see how strong and resilient we are through sports. And it offers us the opportunity to focus on health and wellness as a radical act of self-care. The decision to view our bodies in this way is ultimately up to us.

It has taken me years to rethink my relationship to myself through exercise, but I feel like I have come to a soft-landing place. I am currently finding joy in an approach that incorporates overall body balance and elements of dance, which both brings me back to my love of dance in childhood and makes me laugh as my teen boys cringe at my moves. I am careful not to over train. I know my body and listen to it now. It tells me when I am on the verge of an injury. I know when I am too tired or just feeling unwell and need to skip a day. I take plenty of days and weeks off to let my body recover and rest. I prioritize movement and consider it to be a "nonnegotiable." It regulates my sleep and my appetite. It keeps the aches and pains of middle age at bay. It gives me energy, motivation, and endless inspiration. It vastly improves my mood and helps me to cope with the challenges of my life and my job. And it serves as a constant reminder of how lucky I am to have a healthy, functioning physical self. I know enough to know that a perfect body obtained through exercise just doesn't exist and that it's just not worth the self-loathing and negativity to try to get there.

LET'S TALK!

Know your "why" for exercise! Does it give you more energy? Better sleep? Is it inspiring? Challenge the belief that exercise needs to be about caloric burn or to "undo" something that you have eaten.

No locker-room talk. Celebrate athleticism at all sizes and shapes. No comparing or trying to fit a particular sport's "desired" body type.

Develop an "attitude of gratitude." Think of all the ways that your body can move—what it can do, how strong it is or can become. Stop thinking about exercise in terms of how your body looks, and instead think about what it allows you to do.

Consciously choose for exercise to be empowering rather than disempowering. Don't go to gyms that focus on weight and appearance. Don't participate in talk during class about dieting and losing weight.

Seek out strong, athletic role models who inspire you because of what they have accomplished rather than how they look.

"I really like that, when I'm playing a sport that I love, I can get better at it, and I feel like I can get stronger. I love that feeling that I can smash a ball over the net. It's more about what you can do with your body rather than what it looks like. When you are playing a team sport, it matters how you can work together to get the ball over the net or win the game."

— ELLIE, 12

6

AMAL SAYS

"A Story of Young Adulthood"

"It's still a struggle. I felt controlled by it for a long time, but I have control over it now. I feel far more liberated now."

———————————

At age twenty-four, Amal found herself divorced and seeking help for how to move forward in her life. "I would say that I am a lot more comfortable now sharing about my journey with my body. I have been in therapy for the past year, and I didn't go to therapy specifically for body image, but I realize that a lot of what I did in the past and a lot of how I think about certain things all tie back to my body. It's been a hard journey."

The process of therapy has opened her up to how messages in childhood and experiences in high school set her on a path that she is now trying to course-correct. "I didn't grow up hearing that my body was worthy and valuable, which it is. But at some point in your life, other people that have no relationship to you somehow put this quantifiable worth on your body. It's like 'Now you're worth something because your body looks a certain way or you weigh a certain amount, we can put this value on it now.' And if you don't fit that image, you are seen as less important, even if you have so much more to provide that has nothing to do with your body. That was so hard for me to wrap my head around."

Like so many young women, high school was the time that Amal really started to struggle with trying to fit in with society's ideals for her body and her worth. "I was overweight for the first half of high school. I remember that my father, who is a physician, would make slight comments about how I fit into clothing or what I was eating. I went from eating cereal for breakfast to him making me green juices. I didn't realize how much that fed into things for me. As much as he was trying to turn me into a healthier person, the way it came off was so unhealthy, because it fed me this message of 'You'd better be skinnier before you grow up and move on in this world. You need to prove something to this world.' In reality, I know that it wasn't the case. But that's still how it felt."

Feeling the pressure and jumping on the bandwagon to get "healthier," Amal found herself changing her habits. In addition to daily workouts in gym class, Amal added hot yoga before school and heavy cardio after school, all the while barely eating during the day. She started skipping lunch altogether. The weight started to come off, and, for the first time in her life, she felt like she was experiencing the "perks" of fitting in. Amal soon found herself fielding invites to the Friday night football games, social gatherings, and making more friends. "I started to think that the thinner I was, I was somehow more worthy. The fixation with my weight had a lot to do with self-worth. I started to believe that the lower the number was, [the more that] I was worth people's time and I had more value. It didn't matter how successful I was or how well I was doing in school. In my mind, I was getting skinnier, and it seemed to be paying off."

Amal started college and felt that her issues with her body "followed" her there. She found

"I started to think that the thinner I was, I was somehow more worthy. The fixation with my weight had a lot to do with self-worth. I started to believe that the lower the number was, [the more that] I was worth people's time and I had more value. It didn't matter how successful I was or how well I was doing in school. In my mind, I was getting skinnier, and it seemed to be paying off."

herself dieting, then not dieting. Losing weight, then gaining weight. She began what she describes as "a cycle of losing my worth, finding my worth. It always came back to the number on the scale." She graduated college, started her professional career, got married, got divorced, and then found herself talking in therapy about what had happened in her life up to that point and how she had felt all along the way. She realizes now that her worth has nothing to do with the number on the scale and has started making connections between her choices in life and her relationship to her body.

Having delved into her past, her emotions, and her self-image, Amal can see now that the seeds of her low self-esteem were planted far earlier than high school, when the weight loss behaviors and efforts began to take root. Amal's family is from the Middle East, and, while she was born in the United States, as a young girl, she spent a lot of time in her parent's native country. She describes the cultural message she internalized in those years in terms of her self-image. "Women cover themselves back home, whether it's their hair or their body. The way it's covered, you can't even see their silhouette. It was ingrained in me for religious reasons, but it never sat well with me from the standpoint of a woman and her self-image. I felt like, 'Why are we shamed into hiding our bodies?' I was told that I was not allowed to wear something form-fitting because men will stare. I was told my parents will be disappointed. The message was, 'If you ever talk about your body or show your body, you are going to get shamed, embarrassed, and humiliated.' It took a toll on my mental health and body image because of the amount of guilt and shame that came from just being a woman. I felt that all from a very young age. Once I came to The United States, I was surrounded by a lot of girls who were athletes. They were fit and tiny, and they were getting a lot of attention at school. I wasn't athletic, and it made me feel so worthless, because I wasn't as tiny as all of those other girls. Here in the United States, you can show your body. You can talk about empowerment. But you can still be shamed for it. There, in the Middle East, you can't do any of that, and you will still be shamed for it. It's very different, but also very much the same. You come to realize that it almost feels like no matter where you are in the world, women just have to suffer in their relationships to their bodies."

The therapy that Amal sought out in her early twenties seemed to be the key that unlocked so much pent-up confusion, guilt, and shame. "I feel like I am in a better place where I can talk about it. I feel like it's important to talk about how we feel about our bodies. I didn't grow up talking about that. It was very 'hush, hush,' and I wish that I had people around me that shared in that conversation. Staying quiet for too long puts the shame on it that doesn't deserve to be there. It's always so heartbreaking when I sit down with someone else and hear them talk about their bodies in a negative way. I did that for the longest time, and I didn't treat my body well, which is worse. I can stand in the mirror and say to myself that 'I'm beautiful' a hundred times. But if I'm not going to treat my body that way, I am not going to believe it, because I am not going to take the time to do the things that remind me that my body is valuable the way that it is. It is a conversation that needs to be had. But there is also a lot of action that women need to take."

In asking her about those action steps that she takes now to shift her mindset and behaviors to a more accepting and positive place, Amal is quick to debunk the current way that "self-care" is talked about for women. "I see a lot of things that talk to women today about self-care, which always somehow involves eating chocolate or having a glass of wine. That's fantastic. But what people don't realize is that self-care can sometimes be so ugly. It can be the hardest process. Self-care is sometimes having to cut someone out, because they are not good for my mental health. Self-care is seeing that maybe I need to revamp the way that I look at food—not just what I eat, but the way that I look at it. Those small things—like having chocolate or having a burger—I don't consider those things as self-care. Because it's almost like saying, 'These are moments where we are escaping our reality.' I don't want to escape my reality. I don't want to have every Friday night be the time where I need to escape from how I feel about myself and indulge myself in something else, because, come Saturday, I am still the same person. Loving yourself isn't easy. But you can come out on the other end. Because then you realize that you have so much to offer that has nothing to do with your body."

Amal shares her belief that doing inner work is an ongoing life journey for women, with less of a destination and more of a process, and one that is worth the pain. "I am working through that now, and I think that's always going to be something I am working through. I have many years ahead of me, and there will be other things that I have to work through. I think it's important to know that you have yourself at the end of the day. You have your body. You love yourself. Everything else is a battle that you can conquer. If you don't love yourself, if you don't appreciate yourself, if you aren't taking care of yourself—mind, body, and soul—then good luck getting through anything that comes your way. Because it's going to feel like you are just drowning all of the time. And that's a lot of my story with how I look at my body now. It's about my worth. I feel like I can tackle the world ahead of me. It had nothing to do with the number on the scale."

REFLECTION TIME

When Amal shared her story, what thoughts did you have about your own experiences?
   Where have you felt like you didn't belong? Looking back, do you still feel that way?
   How are you doing with self-care? Do you feel guilty? Does it feel like an indulgence?
   Do you relate to Amal describing the "hard parts" of self-care, such as setting boundaries, making life changes, or dealing with uncomfortable issues?

7

RED LIPSTICK

"The Impact of Beauty and Fashion"

We buried my grandma at the age of ninety-two, with a tube of lipstick in her hand.

When I was a little girl growing up in Ohio, spending time at my grandma's was my first introduction into the world of "beauty." She had been a hairdresser in the years before she married; and, when I was older, she told me stories of gabbing with her clients about all of the men away fighting in World War II, including my grandpa. His picture was always tucked inside the frame of her mirror while she worked. It's interesting to me now to imagine that world: the women keeping up with all of their daily beauty rituals, all the while, their men were off fighting in a brutal and bloody war.

Like so many women of that generation, my grandma stopped working full time when her children were born and took to raising them instead. But her love of all things beauty lingered, and tucked away in the basement were the remnants of her career that she still dusted off from time to time to give someone a perm or do a neighbor's hair. Down the stairs and around the corner from the kitchen, I would find myself, as a young girl, playing with the hair dryer that, by then, sat dormant. It was one of those old-fashioned ones, chair attached, with the vented dryer and the shiny metallic cap. I used to poke around down there all the time, messing with her collection of assorted bobby pins and hairbrushes. I would wind my hair up so tight in her piles of spongy, pink curlers—waiting to unfurl soft, wavy ringlets, hoping to feel as if I had magically stepped out of a fairy tale.

It wasn't just the hair. There was also makeup. My grandma was a Mary Kay® fanatic, and I can remember all the lovely little palettes that I would find when rummaging around in her bathroom. It was all so pretty. It all seemed so glamorous. I was mesmerized.

As girls, our fascination with "beauty" starts young. Early on, little girls are steeped in messages about what it means to be "pretty." All these years later, having succumbed to my own insecurities about my appearance, as well as seeing the toll that it has taken on so many other girls and women, it's easy to malign the beauty and fashion industries for their role in propagating ideals and standards that are toxic to girls and women. The anger and the outcry against them are well deserved in my opinion. They have earned the wrath of those crying out for change, no longer wanting to add to the masses of those who have fallen prey to their manipulation and oppression. Both the fashion and beauty industries have blood on their hands.

But the bottom line on the economy due to the booming success of the fashion and beauty industry is undeniable, and commerce would—without question—come to a grinding halt if one day women would wake up feeling naturally beautiful. These industries net billions of dollars a year and aren't going anywhere any time soon. Women's never-ending quest for beauty is here to stay, and part of me wants to rail against all of this. And yet . . . I love red lipstick. I like to put together outfits. I make it a point to take good care of my skin as I age. Am I being duped? Am I part of the problem? Or am I, like many women, just trying to find a way to embrace the more

empowering and creative aspects that the beauty and fashion industry has to offer while, at the same time, not falling victim to the belief that I am not "enough"?

Katt, age forty-six, is the owner of a highly successful skincare spa in the suburbs of Chicago. She has established herself at the top of her industry, building a business based on helping women feel empowered rather than feeling like they are working against Mother Nature and the hands of time. Katt has not only built an incredible business of loyal followers who need to book sometimes a year in advance, she is also establishing herself as a coach and mentor for other women within the industry to reach the heights of success by focusing on empowerment, charity, and self-love.

Katt started her career as a makeup artist in Hollywood in her twenties, working with top celebrities and the movie star elite. We tend to be obsessed with celebrity culture, and the idea of rubbing elbows with stars that light up the silver screen and grace the cover of magazines is the stuff of dreams for many girls. When sharing what it's really like being up close and personal with those that the rest of us are killing ourselves to look like, Katt gets choked up, sharing that they, too, are "killing themselves to be that. It was heartbreaking to see."

Katt is open about the lessons that she has learned and the ways that they woke her up to the distorted lens through which we see celebrity culture. "As a makeup artist, your job is to make sure that everyone looks perfect. But after a while, you realize that what you are really doing is making sure that you are fixing people's mascara after they have thrown up their lunch, or you are trying to hide with lipstick the darkness of their teeth, because they have worn the enamel off of them from purging their food. I was getting the opportunity to be around people I had looked up to my whole life. Some of these actors and actresses were in movies that I had watched growing up. For me, at that time, it was like the curtain was pulled back. I realized that what I had been idolizing and trying to be like was, in reality, someone who was more lost and more broken than I ever could have imagined. That, for me, was so shocking, to discover that the best thing that could happen would be to miss entirely what you thought you were shooting for."

At the peak of her career, Katt decided that she no longer wanted to work in that environment, and instead moved across the country and settled in the Midwest, starting all over again. This time, however, she decided that, rather than put makeup on her clients in order to make them feel beautiful, it was going to become her job to help them take it off. "I think that women are the most beautiful when they are the most vulnerable. Makeup, beauty, and hair are our shields. Working in skincare, I take away the makeup and the fabulous wardrobe, and wrap someone up on the table, and I start to see their strength and personality come through. I get to see the true essence of that person, and I just think that's so beautiful. As women, we waste so much time having conversations about our shoes or our [purses], but the second that we take all that away, the conversation becomes about big heavy topics that are supposed to be taboo, but reveal the intellectual parts of a woman, and I love that. It allows women to be powerful. All of the perfectionism and controlling everything, when you take that away, that's when you're really strong."

Katt goes on to talk further about the messages from within her industry that focus entirely on a woman's outward appearance without any context for what is on the inside. "Women are told not to use our voice. It's kind of like saying, 'We don't need your brains. We don't need that here.' And it sucks. And what sucks even more is that we do it to each other. As women, we don't dress for men. We dress for other women, and we pigeonhole ourselves in that way. That's the fun thing about being in beauty the way that I am in beauty, which is that, within the constructs of this really detrimental industry toward women, I can tell women, 'Hey it's okay. You want to scream something from the top of the mountain? You can do it.'"

In addition to the silencing of women, Katt feels strongly that the beauty industry focuses heavily on women being seen as sex objects. "I would like to see the beauty industry start to leave that word, sexy, out. We always objectify women, and women objectify themselves. When I was in middle school, I remember reading a Cosmo Magazine article outlining '100 Ways to Be Sexy.' I think that the beauty industry needs to stop putting so much emphasis on our biological function as women, which is about sex. When we start looking at women who are strong and

"Your body
is not a trend;
and perpetuating
that it is,
is damaging."

— MARY, 36

beautiful, like Ruth Bader Ginsburg, we see that their beauty is about what comes out of them rather than what we can put on them."

In an industry known for promoting youth and fighting the effects of aging at literally all costs, Katt is adamant that the industry needs to shift on this point as well. "In terms of aging, we are always worried about what is degrading and what is falling apart. We have this obsession with getting rid of wrinkles. Our faces, as we age, tell the story of how we have lived—the expressions that we make when we smile. I have a wrinkle that goes across my forehead that I love, because it reflects back an expression that I make when I am happy for someone. The beauty industry will tell me I need to Botox it. But I don't want to Botox it! It doesn't all need to go away; we just need to reframe it and talk about it in a different way. I think that we need to meet people where they are at, be present with them, and not superimpose a predetermined version of beauty on them. We are human, we are different, we all have things about us that aren't perfect. That's what makes you unique. That's what makes you you."

Twelve-year-old Daniela shares, "To me, pretty is your attitude to other people and how you react to things. Pretty is being nice to people, and being kind, and helping out." Sadly, it's not just the beauty industry that modern girls and women need to reconcile their relationships with. The fashion industry is also an often-maligned and much-deserving target of wrath when it comes to how it's branding and messaging to girls and women profits by feeding society unrealistic standards, ideals, and pressures to consume.

Shana, thirty-eight years old, lives in New York and has worked with top designers in the fashion industry for years. As a teen, "fashion" to Shana meant looking through J Crew catalogs and cruising the mall. "I was a tomboy who liked borrowing my brother's clothes. I liked art and making things as much as I liked science and math, but at that time, clothes weren't a creative outlet." Being an intrinsically creative and artistic person, Shana feels like that all started to change when she went away to college.

As she pursued her college degree, Shana says, "I found myself caring more about the clothes that I bought and whether they fit well and reflected my personality. I think the most ironic thing is that I decided to pursue fashion while I was in eating disorder treatment." As she was undergoing treatment, Shana found that, by no longer thinking all the time about food, weight, and her body, she began to realize how much more creative potential she had. "Once I was no longer counting calories or worrying about weight, I suddenly had a lot of time on my hands. And as someone who has always enjoyed making things with my hands, I began sewing clothes. I started taking old clothes apart and putting them back together, figuring out how they were made. There is a surprising amount of math involved in fashion, particularly pattern making. So, it was sort of a natural extension for me."

Shana admits that while the development of her eating disorder was complex and multifaceted, comparing herself to catalog models and cover girls on magazines, like Shape, did make an impact. "I sort of obsessed over the differences in how my body compared to theirs. And I do think all of this directly played a role in the development of my eating disorder. Now that everyone has Instagram and other social media, I think that we're all much more keenly aware that things are not always as they appear. But in the '90s, I don't think it was as widely known just how many photos were being airbrushed, and how much things were being photoshopped. I took everything at face value. And when I saw the way that models, athletes, and actresses looked, I told myself that if I just worked hard enough, I could look the same way that they did."

Looking back on it now, Shana can see all of the complexities that began to form her relationship to her physical appearance as a young girl and a teen. "My mom is someone who never explicitly said anything about how a woman's body should look, and nothing was ever centered around weight at home. But my mom was always dressed and in full makeup anytime she left the house. I can remember her saying, 'You never know who you might see!'—which pretty much sums up her belief in always putting your best image forward. I never once saw her leave the house without her hair, makeup, and nails done, and she was always put-together in terms of clothes. You certainly would never see her leave the house in loungewear, and I don't think that I saw her even go out to the end of the driveway to pick up the newspaper in her pajamas! I think a lot of this expectation surrounding image was passed down from my mom's mom. She is also very much attuned to her image and how she is being perceived by others. My grandma can remember, and will tell you, without you even asking, how much she weighed in 1986, down to the pound. But while my mom is someone who is attuned to how her clothes fit and whether or not she has been 'eating badly,' her relationship with food seems pretty normal. She is generally very balanced and doesn't deprive herself or skip meals and food does not seem to dominate the conversation or her thoughts."

Now, having fully recovered, Shana sees fashion and her work in the industry as an extension of her creativity and her resourcefulness and credits her love of fashion as a part of her recovery. "The years that I was in treatment were incredibly inventive for me. I would buy random clothing patterns on the Internet or a local JOANN and make things just to make them. Once I started wearing what I made, people would ask if I was selling items. I started making clothes for friends and friends of friends." With a newfound sense of excitement and purpose for her life, Shana began reaching out to friends in the music and fashion industry. She was offered the opportunity to work as a freelancer for companies like Levi's, making custom clothing for musicians and other performance artists at live shows and festivals.

Years later, with her feet firmly planted successfully within this tough and often brutal industry, Shana has a lot to say about fashion and its responsibility to reach women on a real and empowering level. "This industry still has a long way to go. We're by no means 'there' when it comes to the acceptance of different body types or skin colors. But I will say a lot has changed since the '90s and '00s. I find that more brands are getting into extended size offerings, because large retailers are requiring it and see that there is a consumer with money who they've been ignoring for years. But even so, in the past, brands would not have touched extended sizing." When asked about the "standard sizing," which is considered "ideal" by the industry, Shana reports, "The majority of us have not been taught how to design for or fit for someone who falls outside of the range of 5'9" tall and 34"-27"-36" measurement. That is the 'standard.' "

"I think beauty means the way that God created you, and God created everything. I don't think it means clothes and makeup."

— EVELYN, 10

She does, however, as an insider, offer hope that it is beginning to change. Shana points to brands that are dedicated to showcasing diversity amongst women and body types. She also points to the changing demographics in the consumer base, noting that "Gen Z will flat out disregard, and never come back to, brands that are not inclusive or diverse. It's not even up for debate. I think we're also seeing a big uptick in plus-size influencers and 'everyday women' on Instagram and other platforms. Young people are having more fun with second-hand and used clothing, and they care about their environmental impact, so that changes things as well. They're taking more chances and being more creative with clothes. I think fashion is markedly more fun now. There are so many ways for young people to enjoy clothes, and when you see brands and influencers wearing used clothing and reflecting all different body types, it's more inspiring and feels more approachable."

When talking about how to be body confident in an industry steeped in toxic messages for women, Shana shares, "I think age helps and the fact that I've been recovered as long as I have. It's funny, when I'm in fittings, I don't even think about how my body compares to a model's. Maybe it's because, when I was anorexic, even at my smallest I never looked like a model. Because my body is just not built like theirs. I told myself when I was younger that I could look like them if I just worked hard enough. Well, I did that, and it didn't work. And my life was miserable. I just don't even go down that road anymore. And I don't beat myself up for not looking like others, because I don't compare myself in the first place. I feel comfortable, confident, and strong as the person who I currently am, so why would I want to change that?"

At the end of the day, the beauty and fashion industries do have a massive part to play in the disempowerment of women and the ways that they manipulate girls and women to part with their pennies and give in to the trends that are constantly changing and never truly attainable. And yes, these industries do have a way to go. But women like Katt and Shana are paving the way for a more savvy, confident, and culture-changing consumer base.

In my own life, I have come to believe that fashion can be an extension of who we are, our creativity, and our identity. It can be a fun and playful way to introduce ourselves to the world. Engaging in self-care through beauty rituals and enhancing what we feel are our physical attributes and assets can be confidence-boosting and esteem-building.

When I think about my grandmother, the color of her hair dye or her lipstick weren't what made her beautiful. What made her beautiful was her loving spirit, the care that she poured into every pot of marinara sauce that she made, and the way that she made me feel. The memories of her that are the most lovely are ultimately not about how she looked but rather about holding her soft hands, hearing her stories, and sitting by her side. And she did, all the way until the end, love a good tube of lipstick. As do I. A bright, sassy-red one.

LET'S TALK!

Be a conscious consumer. Don't shop at stores that promote only one version of beauty or a one-size-fits-all approach. Support vendors that celebrate beauty and diversity in all races, sizes, and shapes.

Confidently walk away. Fashion and beauty aren't your thing? Own it. Don't feel pressured to buy into trends or products just because others are touting them.

Experiment and play around with ways to enhance what features that you love best. Love your hair? Invest in a great cut or some fun styling products. Love your eyes? Learn a few tips and tricks to bring out their shape or their color.

Take some time to curate your closet. Only keep items that fit well and that you feel confident in. Wear what you feel good in, and you will feel good throughout your day.

Don't buy into the importance of size. Get rid of all of the "aspirational"-sized items in your closet. Cut out clothing tags that trigger you. Remember, you don't wear the size of your clothing on the outside. No one else knows or cares what size it is!

Don't be afraid to show your style, your personality, and your confidence through your wardrobe, fashion, or makeup choices. Take risks! Be bold and daring!

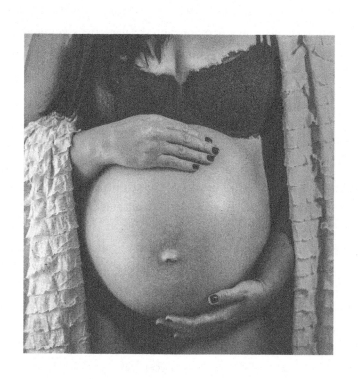

8

MIRROR, MIRROR, ON THE WALL

"Motherhood, Middle Age, and Beyond"

"You carry that baby so well. You look so cute! When I was pregnant, I didn't carry it well at all. Trust me, it was bad. I did not look that cute."

It was an early fall morning. I was sitting at an outdoor table at my local coffee shop, watching as the early Saturday morning crowd was coming and going from the nearby farmer's market. As I sat, I heard this exchange between two women. One might think at first that they were friends, sitting close by, hovered over their coffees, dishing on all things pregnancy related.

This particular exchange, however, happened between two complete strangers. One of them, an unsuspecting, young, and expectant mom leaving the coffee shop, steaming cup in hand. The other, an older woman on her way in and having no issue proclaiming out loud to all of the strangers within earshot that she apparently didn't feel "cute enough" while pregnant.

Two women, passersby. One of them not even flinching to comment about the size, shape, and appearance of the other's body. All said in the spirit of compliment to the one, all the while self-effacing and self-shaming herself. It was as if some twisted sisterhood spirit of motherhood made this all okay. I marveled yet again at the flippancy and normalcy of such words. I marveled at how two men crossing the street would never make an attempt to compliment another man, an absolute stranger, about his body, all the while trash talking his own. Why is this normal? What was that exchange really about?

I know what it's about. A lot of us ladies do. Especially those of us who have been pregnant. I remember looking at family photos when my first son was born and thinking, "I look so puffy." Everyone else in the photos looked great—healthy, perky, and ecstatic at this new little life in our family. Even my newborn son, with his gaze that already signaled his intensity and passion, all the ingredients that had just been baked up—he looked so cute, so vulnerable. Me? My body had been to hell and back bringing him into the world. Yes, I was "puffy." But I was also magnificent. Sadly, I didn't see myself according to that latter description at the time.

Pregnancy and motherhood: What a complex, heart-wrenching, and, often, literally gut-wrenching time of life for women. The minute that we find out we are pregnant, our lives are changed. Our hearts are changed. Our lives don't "bounce back." Our hearts don't "bounce back." Why then have we decided that our bodies have to? Who made this rule? Where does this idea come from?

Tracy, age thirty-one, describes the challenges and struggles of trying to both embrace the joy of pregnancy, but also deal with her body changing rapidly and in ways that are hard. "I was very athletic when I was younger. When I decided to stray away from sports and hit puberty, I gained a lot of weight, and it was very uncomfortable for me. Now again, with pregnancy, it has been challenging. You are growing in places you don't necessarily want to grow. Your clothing

isn't fitting, and the number on the scale keeps going up. Your size is increasing. All of that. I went into pregnancy feeling pretty confident about where I was at physically, plus I really try to take care of myself. I really love food, and I like to enjoy food."

Tracy says that trying to stay mindful and surround herself with positive support has been incredibly helpful. "I've been intentional about making sure that the people that I am around are very supportive and encouraging. I am only focusing back on positive comments like, 'You're glowing,' or 'Relax, don't worry about your weight. Eat that extra cupcake, it's okay.' " She is also trying to manage the number that she sees on the scale when she goes for her prenatal appointments. "You can become kind of fixed on that number. I plan to focus on how to stay active this summer and do some dance classes to have some time to take care of myself after the baby comes. I do have weight in places where I'm not used to carrying weight, so I do sometimes have concerns about where it's going to go, but I'm not overly concerned with thinking about the baby weight right now."

In addition to keeping her focus on impending motherhood rather than impending weight loss worries, Tracy tells me that "Knowing that the baby is growing and is healthy is the best part. It's been kind of a unique experience for me in that I am adopted. This is the first time that I am connected to someone in such a foundational way. To me, it's amazing that, when my daughter is born, she is going to have that connection to me from the get-go, and a lot of that was lost in my biological family. Carrying someone that is going to be connected to me for years to come has been pretty profound. It's pretty inexplicable." Our society, our culture, our medical advancements, and our diet culture have conditioned us. They have conditioned us to believe that we can control our bodies—that we somehow hold the keys, have the ingredients, or should just have the sheer willpower to bend our bodies to our ideals and desires. Nowhere can this belief be more profoundly shattered than when it comes to pregnancy and motherhood. Every day, women are willing their bodies to cooperate in some way; getting pregnant, staying pregnant, having a healthy pregnancy, avoiding complications, having a successful delivery, and then, getting "our bodies back." Carrying a live baby to full term is an incredible miracle, and many women have had heartbreaking experiences in not being able to will their bodies to do so. The pressure that we exert on ourselves to "lose the baby weight" and get back into our pre-pregnancy size as quickly as possible—is that how we repay our bodies?

Those who have just given birth soon find themselves depleted, juggling a whole new reality, caring for and feeding that new little soul, all the while being spoon fed herself a toxic message that she can and must diet and restrict her way back to her pre-baby weight. The demands of new motherhood are never-ending and intense. For the first time, self-care truly becomes a very basic and very challenging reality. Often, and sadly, precious time, energy, and bandwidth are taken up with negative and critical thoughts and feelings of shame about the body that has just performed this incredible feat. This time of new motherhood is so tender. So overwhelming. And, if we are not careful, a time when we can develop some serious patterns to subvert our own most basic needs. While this stage of life can be full of complex body image issues, those pressures don't just apply to women who are in the early stages of motherhood. Those pressures extend to women all throughout adulthood as they traverse middle age and beyond.

There can be a common misconception that once a woman reaches middle age, as if by magic, all of that pressure to live up to certain standards, to control our bodies, will just go away. For some women, approaching middle age and beyond can feel like pulling into safe harbor. This stage, for a lot of women, can finally be a time of caring a little less about what others think, living a little bolder and wiser, a time of "coming home." Sadly though, many other women in mid-life and beyond can still find themselves lost at sea, or may even find the pressures rising.

Motherhood, middle age, and aging in general engulf us all in real-life challenges and issues: Raising our kids. Health issues for ourselves, our spouses, our friends, and our parents. It's a time when life needs us to be most fully present, confident, and able to handle the tasks of the day, all the while sending us a message that we need to stay young, shapely, and pretty. We lay it all on the floor every day for those in our lives, hoping to find some scraps of time to take care of

"One of the biggest issues that women our age face is being too critical of our bodies and ourselves. Our bodies are amazing and life-giving! If only we could see ourselves for the warriors that we are for our families and children. Yes, our bodies do change and evolve, but so too should our minds and our collective views about what 'beauty' is and what our bodies have accomplished as women and mothers."

— TARA, 45

ourselves, which we usually reserve a spot for only at the bottom of the seemingly never-ending to-do list.

A while back, I was at dinner with a group of women, and I once again found myself in conversation about our bodies. The discussion had turned to dating after divorce. A couple of the women—both moms, both amazing—were sharing their stories. The conversation had started to get heavy. These two women had both been through so much. Divorce is full of grief and loss, a reckoning of choices made and things gone wrong and all things unraveling and coming apart in every way. It is heartbreaking and life-altering. It takes parenting to a whole new level, both from the standpoint of helping children understand, grieve, and heal, as well as the ongoing day to day challenges of managing a single-parent home while co-parenting with someone you decided that you could no longer live with. I listened as these two women talked raw and real about their stories, one of them having plucked up the courage to leave because the relationship had been toxic and abusive.

These two women were warriors. They had been through a lot. I saw them as empowered, strong, resilient, and so courageous in the steps that they had taken to reclaim their lives. Instead, the conversation had veered toward plastic surgery, and both women were sharing that they felt like they needed surgery before confidently reentering the dating world. I realized that these women weren't seeing what—or rather, who—I was seeing. Somewhere along the way, these women had ingrained these messages that, in order to fully transform their lives, they first needed to transform their bodies. Why does society continue to send us this message? And why, as women, do we continue to allow ourselves to internalize it?

Donna is fifty. Working full time, being recently divorced, and having raised two kids, she is open about how she feels at this stage of her life. "Overall, I think that aging is looked upon as a bummer. I am starting to feel the effects, and I'm not thrilled. Though I know there are great examples of aging gracefully, since I haven't been good to my body, I'm not in this category. Media, of course, highlights women who remain upbeat, wrinkle-free, cellulite-free, skinny, and athletic. I am always torn between trying to accept my body, which feels like 'giving up,' or trying to fundamentally change eating and exercise habits to feel better about my appearance." Adding a recent divorce into the mix of her life has created an added pressure to think about her appearance. "I have trouble believing that I am attractive, or that my decidedly squishy body would be desirable. How can I expect a guy to like my body if I don't like my body? And frankly, it angers me that society places so much importance on being in a relationship."

According to Donna, her issues with her body—like so many women her age can relate—have been with her for a while now. Donna's body image issues started around seventh grade. A growing and developing young woman at the time, Donna describes a "big bust" that emerged in her teen years and describes feeling self-conscious about it. Often feeling the barbs of teasing from the boys, while at the same time feeling glared at by the girls, Donna learned to wage a war against her body out of concern for how others saw her and how she stacked up against everyone else around her. As is often the case for women in that generation, her mother sent some strong messages. "My mom was not much help. She frequently cautioned me about 'getting fat.' She limited my portion sizes of food and got annoyed when I went for seconds. Meanwhile, my little sister was encouraged to eat as much as possible, as her body didn't start to really bloom until college. The message was that I was 'chubby,' and my sister was 'skinny.' Body image has been an issue for most of my life. I was determined to model the opposite for my girls."

So many moms relate to the struggle of wanting their daughters to forge a different path than the one they themselves know when it comes to body image and issues with food. The reality of how difficult it is to model a value that is still such a personal challenge is something that Donna struggled with even before her kids were born. "When I was in my thirties and pregnant with my kids, I could not really appreciate that I was growing a human or even look in the mirror very often. I hated being so large and hated stretch marks. I hated that my breasts were now twice their size and painful. It makes me sad to think about how I felt about myself. As I lost the weight each time, I tried to remind myself to appreciate my body more. I delivered my kids easily and without medications, nursed them, and remained in relatively good health through-out. But I always reverted back to that mindset of being a 'curvy girl.' "

Despite her own personal battle, Donna was determined to have awareness when it came to raising her girls. "I do remember getting ready to go out, and complaining about how clothes didn't fit, or how I looked in a certain piece of clothing. I'm sure that they overheard this and wondered why I seemed to dislike my body, but I tried to never use the word 'fat' about myself or anyone else. I distinctly remember a comment about a girl in one of my children's elementary classes being 'fat,' and I questioned them on who said that and what they thought it meant. As early as second or third grade, they were aware that some bodies were 'fat' and that this was not a good thing, according to their peers. We had talks about how all bodies are different sizes, and no one should be disparaged because their body is bigger. I'm pretty sure that they wondered why I would say this and then turn around and disparage my own body."

With this growing awareness of how society and culture were sending strong messages to her vulnerable kids, Donna continued in her efforts to promote healthy body image at home as she addressed her own challenges. "When the girls became 'tweens,' I tried harder to limit my own negative self-talk in front of them. At that time, both girls were big fans of all the tween shows, which, of course, starred skinny, mostly blonde girls with expert makeup and hair. These char-acters seemed to have endless clothing options and boyfriends. I mentioned as often as possible that this was not an accurate portrayal of most women. Thankfully, their dad would always back me up on this point and reinforce the message that all bodies are unique and beautiful."

As is true in most families, Donna's girls had different body types. Different proportions. And different interests when it came to sports and extracurricular activities. Donna worked hard to pay attention, listen, discuss, praise, and in general be a sounding board for her daughters growing up, especially when it came to issues about their weight and bodies. In overhearing a conversation amongst her teen daughter and her friends at the time about how 'fat' they were

"For me, it was my mother. It stems from that. Maybe she didn't have a good self-image. I felt like a scapegoat for her insecurities. I remember one day when I was a freshman in high school and was getting ready to go out with my cousins, and one of my cousins was so brilliant and so gifted intellectually. I was in the bedroom getting ready, and my mom came in and said, 'You can't wear that. I want you to wear your Gloria Vanderbilt jeans and your purple sweater.' When I asked her why, she said, 'I have just sat through a whole conversation with your aunt and uncle about how brilliant your cousin is. Since I can't have that same conversation about you, I want you to be dressed in your best outfit.' I remember it breaking something. I remember that exact moment, because it cemented this belief that I have nothing worthwhile to offer. It became all about how I 'look.'"

— DEBORAH, 54

all feeling, Donna tried later to talk to her about it privately and was told, "That's just how we talk to each other, Mom, it's no big deal (eye roll)!"

As she navigated these turbulent waters with her teens, Donna remained vigilant, steadfast, and open with her girls. Recently, one of her daughters, now in college, has become quite strict and rigid with herself around food and exercise. She has also recently reached out to her mom to ask for help in finding a therapist who specializes in body image issues. Donna is more than happy to help, in the hopes that her daughter can suffer far less than she has over the years with feelings of self-hatred and self-doubt. When Donna is asked what does make her feel confident now as a woman in middle age—trying to accept and make peace with her body and her life now—she shares her long list of affirmations with me:

I feel confident when I play tennis and return a tough shot.

I feel confident when I make it through a level two yoga class.

I feel confident when I have maintained better eating habits.

I feel confident when I'm working, since no one else in the company can do my job.

I feel confident when my kids want to spend time with me and each other.

I feel confident when I pay my own mortgage and bills and take my kids out to dinner because I want to.

I feel confident when I wear heels, eyeliner, and my favorite bra.

I feel confident when I assemble something, or fix something in my house, or even change lightbulbs.

I feel confident when I learn something new.

Divorce and stressful events are not the only issues that can have women grappling to control their bodies in middle age. By far, one of the biggest issues affecting women's relationships to their bodies at this stage of life is coming to terms with serious health issues, sometimes overnight altering their life and their views on aging. For many women, one health issue in particular is seemingly running rampant, affecting women's physical, emotional, and spiritual well-being as well as their body image in every way.

In the spring of 2019, Melanie, age forty-three, had an abnormal mammogram. What seemed like a lump that was "highly suspicious" was biopsied and quickly diagnosed as stage two breast cancer with ductal carcinoma in situ. Further testing and cancer-positive lymph nodes meant a change to stage three and a treatment plan that included chemo, then a double mastectomy, followed by radiation. Melanie says that opting for the double mastectomy was, in part, due to fear of the cancer coming back on the other side of her body as well as also wanting more symmetrical features.

Almost two years later and cancer-free, Melanie says she is "grateful to be alive and on the other side of it," but finds that the issues related to her body image after cancer still bother her. Melanie says that one of the most upsetting things is no longer having a nipple on her right side, due to how close the DCIS was to the surface of her skin. She says that her husband always tells her it's "not a big deal" and that he still thinks she's beautiful. It bothers her though, especially knowing that she had waited a couple of years in between mammograms and that "maybe they could have caught it earlier."

In general, Melanie says her body feels like it has "battle scars," and she finds herself stressed at the thought of buying a swimsuit to wear on vacation and to the pool this summer. In addition to the scars, Melanie says that radiation left part of her skin near her chest darker than the other side. She also speaks of the myriad of decisions that needed to be made throughout her journey about her body, and how friends who are also survivors have had to face similar decisions. Do you get implants? Do you get a prosthetic? Melanie decided yes to the implants due to wanting to have "regular-looking female parts." While some of her friends opted for prosthetics, Melanie says that she still felt young enough to justify surgery and wanted her body to "look like other women." After radiation, Melanie had her second reconstructive surgery, which included fat grafting, taking skin from her legs for more of a "natural look" for her breasts, but resulting in more scarring on her body.

Shortly after treatment, Melanie met another woman in the community who was also battling breast cancer. Heather was diagnosed at thirty-six years old with a very aggressive and quick-moving HER2 type of cancer. She tells me there were three lumps in her naturally large and dense breasts. Heather opted for a double mastectomy and has undergone multiple surgeries. Heather tells me that body image issues have plagued her on and off since her twenties, when a family member made a comment about her having "cankles" or large ankles. "When I was diagnosed, I was playing tennis four times a week and was pretty fit. At the time, I would have told you that I was twenty pounds overweight. Now I would die to get back down to that weight."

Heather also shares the very real stress of losing hair with chemotherapy and how that impacts self-image and self-confidence. "When I heard cancer, all I thought right away was, 'Oh my gosh, I am going to lose my hair.' It's wild that you become more scared of your hair being gone for a significant amount of time than the illness itself. I think that says a lot about how society relates to looks too. That you have something that is trying to kill you and you have hair on your head, and they are equally as scary. That's ridiculous. No matter how much you tell yourself, 'It's just hair,' it's how you see yourself, it's how you identify. The hair issue is a really huge piece that I don't think people talk enough about when you have cancer."

In addition to changes to the breasts themselves and hair loss for many women, breast cancer treatment often also brings with it concerns about weight gain due to medications and loss of physical activity. Melanie says she struggled with this too. "I was very active before this happened. Last summer, I managed to play golf, but I've had several surgeries, and, each time, I've needed to take a break from activity for my body to heal. Each time, I was back to square one with fitness. Right now, I am just trying to walk to get some steps in and start to get my fitness back slowly."

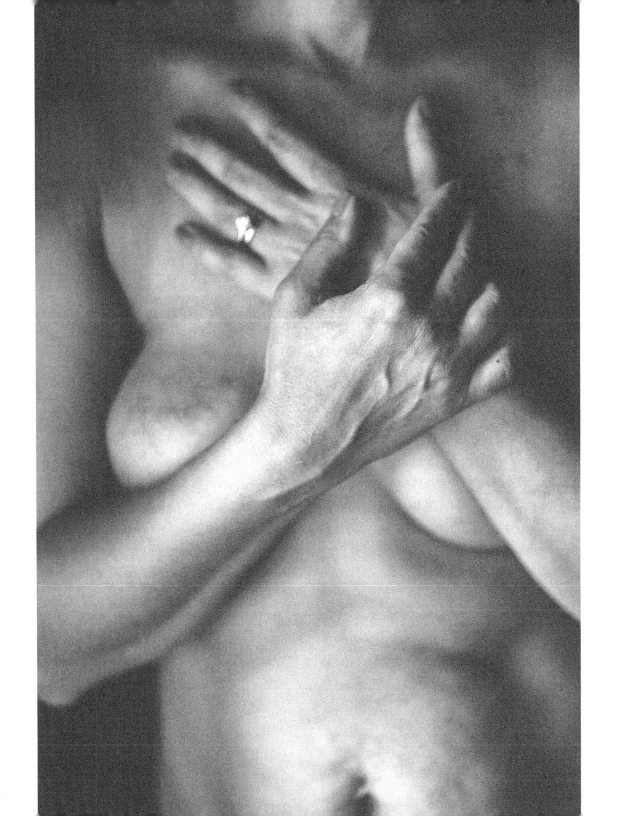

Both Melanie and Heather are adjusting to life after cancer and the myriad of changes with their bodies. Stating more than once that she is "lucky to be alive," Melanie feels conflicted about the life-threatening disease that ravaged her body yet left her still feeling self-conscious about the visible reminders and changes to her body that she has endured. "These breasts don't feel like 'mine.' Sometimes, I just feel differently. They are nicer shaped now than they were after breastfeeding three kids. Maybe something positive has come out of it. Before breast cancer, I was more worried about how my whole body looked. Now I am more focused on just staying healthy and following doctor's orders. I have been less worried about how everything looks, but I still want to feel 'normal,' which is why I made the decision to cold cap so that I didn't lose all my hair and have some semblance of a 'normal life.' " While Melanie was able to keep most of her hair throughout her chemotherapy treatments, she did lose her eyelashes and eyebrows, which she admits was hard. "The craze now is all about eyelashes, and I had none."

Heather, too, reflects now on how having had cancer has impacted her and her relationship to her body. "I have lost trust and faith in my body and its ability to heal. I do not trust it moving forward. I do things now to prove that my body can do it, but overarching, I do not have a good relationship with my body. I look at how it has failed me. However, I also know that I need to flip that on its head. Because I did survive cancer. I have recovered from many surgeries. I have lost weight. I have gained it back. At this point in my life, being forty-one going through these things, I need to remind myself that I am still here because my body has served me and my body has survived. And while it has faltered, it has not failed. It's a dichotomy of what I feel and what I know. And what I feel is very different from what I know. Rectifying that is a struggle on a daily basis for me."

Melanie and Heather's brave journeys shed light on how, for so many women, body image takes a toll through deep struggles that compete with the gratitude to be alive and well, but still acknowledge the difficulty of loss of control and the desire to be seen as "normal and beautiful." Cathy, in her sixties, is also a breast cancer survivor, and she says, "When you are bald as a jellybean, you just don't sweat the small stuff. Having breast cancer at age forty put in perspective that my body is just one part of my life. It was a good lesson to learn then; so, as I have gotten older, I have tried to use that. If I notice more wrinkles or things changing or my hair getting more gray, I just try to remember that it's one small thing. It's just one part of me, and it's a natural process, and it's going to happen. In the bigger picture, the people that love me are going to love me if I have 10,000 wrinkles."

"I look so old." Who is this person looking at me in the mirror? Surely, it's not me. How does this happen so quickly? And what are these weird changes that I am feeling in my body and seeing in the mirror? Seemingly overnight, my face looks more jowly. A little heavier. My waistline is thickening. I know that hormones, those tricky little buggers, are signaling that, yet again, a change is on the horizon, ushering in yet another stage of my life. Suddenly, I feel like the queen in "Snow White," looking into the mirror, pleading the question, "Am I still fair? That girl walking in the woods is younger, thinner, prettier." I know the queen in the story is an evil villain. And yet, on some level, I can kind of relate. Aging and the pressure to stay young and beautiful are very real.

For far too long, aging has been seen in such a negative light, but the reality is that most women will tell you that along with more candles on the cake also comes more wisdom, more perspective, and a greater appreciation for life itself. My body has traversed pregnancy and new motherhood. It carries me now through the looming teen years as a mom. Middle age. Getting older. It's all here, and it's all happening now. I know that I cannot turn back the hands of the clock. I can't even stand on them long enough for me to feel like time is moving at a reasonably leisurely pace. On social media, through my television, at lunch with friends, the conversations about staying young, thin, fit, and beautiful surround me daily. Daily. Every day is a choice. How can we frame our changing bodies with motherhood? How can we rethink our issues with aging? Not every woman gets to age. It's a privilege. I want to age well. I know that I will struggle with it. I've accepted that I may not always approach it with grace and dignity, but I can commit to doing my best. I can commit to taking care of my health and my skin and, most importantly, staying in touch with that deepest self, which knows no age, no bounds, and no limits.

LET'S TALK!

Whether it's pregnancy, middle age, or beyond, focus on gratitude for what your body has done for you and what it can continue to do for you.

Seek out role models of women your age or older whom you admire and who inspire you.

Challenge the belief that our bodies need to "bounce back" after pregnancy or that we need to "fight the signs of aging!"

Don't participate in negative conversations about women's bodies as they go through the stages of pregnancy or later life issues. Shut those negative communications down and instead encourage the conversation to focus on a more positive spin, or change the topic of conversation altogether.

Compliment other women based on what they do, a specific attribute, or a quality about them that you admire rather than praising or focusing on their appearance.

Think of aging as a privilege not a curse. Not everyone gets to see another birthday or rack up candles on their cake.

When you struggle with the effects of aging on your body or your appearance, choose to think about the wisdom, the relationships, and the memories that you have accumulated instead.

If going through a medical issue or having a personal crisis, find someone who can support you, or seek counseling or therapy.

"I stopped coloring my hair when I was in my forties. Now I really like my gray hair. I have worked hard for each and every one of these gray hairs. I feel the same way about my wrinkles. To me, wrinkles aren't anything to be afraid of, because it shows a life lived. And that's something to be celebrated. That whole 'growing old gracefully' is about having the grace for yourself. My eyes are droopy, I've got the jowls, but it's okay. I have made some bad choices in this life, but I have also made some good choices in this life. It is what it is. And that's what the gray hairs and the wrinkles represent to me, and I'm proud of it."

— KATHLEEN, 54

9

TERRI SAYS

"A Story of Late Adulthood"

"**Body consciousness** always has and continues to be what defines my way of thinking, good or bad."

_____

Terri is sixty-two years old. Reflecting back on her life so far, she is open about how much of that life has been consumed by thoughts about her body and her weight, starting at an early age. "I grew up in an era of Barbie dolls with their beautiful figures. I remember playing with them for hours with my best childhood friend. I don't have a Barbie doll figure, but it was so nice to imagine that I was her. I grew up in the '50s, when there was a very specific dress type and body type that was considered ideal."

Terri describes what life was like for her in college when her issues with her body really began to affect her life. "I studied quite a bit and didn't have much time for physical activity. Actually, around the time I was in college, unless you were a gymnast, a dancer, or were studying to be a physical education teacher, there weren't a lot of options that I was aware of for keeping physically fit. It's not like today. So, I studied and studied, and ate while I studied."

Falling into some patterns of mindless snacking, eating while studying, and in general enjoying larger quantities of "things like popcorn," Terri realized that she had started to gain weight. "I'm not and never have been a large woman, but I started putting on weight and this bothered me. So, one day I decided to try to figure out how to purge so that I could expunge what I had eaten." It became a habit quickly, despite the secrecy, shame, guilt, and physical danger that surrounds this behavior pattern. She began to feel like she had found some sort of solution to a problem that had plagued her since the days of dreaming as a girl that maybe, one day, she could in fact look like Barbie. "So, that solved the problem of the extra weight because I could just study, eat, vomit, repeat. I actually started feeling pretty good about myself because I was getting thinner, and so, my clothes got easier to put on. The only problem was finding a way to hide this from my family, because I was still living with them and sharing one of the common bathrooms with everybody. I had heard stories about anorexia and bulimia while in college, and I remember thinking that my situation was controllable. I liked how I looked, I had energy, it was all good."

Reinforced by the addiction that is bulimia and the intoxication of feeling "in control" of her body in a way that is reinforced by society and cultural pressures, Terri found herself in early adulthood, always looking for opportunities to engage in this unnatural way of forcing her body to inhabit a smaller size. When she started her first job, Terri found herself in an office environment every day, making it harder to engage in her behaviors during the day. At a time in life when her career began to take root, her days at work were peppered with intense thoughts and anxieties about how to still use behaviors, how to make sure she wasn't eating too much during the day, in the event that she would get caught purging at work, and in general, obsessing about

her body. Her life had become a vicious cycle of obsessions and behaviors that were psychologically toxic, physically unhealthy, secretive, and, ultimately, dangerous.

Without anyone knowing of this secret struggle, life for Terri went on and the issues of young adulthood, such as starting her career, relationships, and starting a family, all co-mingled with this private, self-defeating war going on inside of herself. "I had met my first husband while in college, and we married about a year after I had graduated. He knew I stressed out about food, but I don't think he knew what I was doing. He never said anything about my body one way or the other. When I became pregnant with my first child, that was the first time I really took a pause in my behavior. At that time in my mind, thinking about any damage to my own body was inconsequential, but risking the health of my unborn baby was not something I could or would do. I ate normally and kept my impulses in check. And wow! That was hard to do! I gained more weight with that pregnancy than what I was reading at the time I was 'supposed to.' Emotionally, I was a wreck about that. After my first baby was born, I wanted to lose that extra weight. I reverted back to my old habits."

Terri describes how life took on a new "normal"—working full time, caring for her new baby, making meals, and running a household. As any new mom can relate, the plate is full at this stage, and depleting the body can exacerbate emotions and fear of losing control. Looking back on it now, Terri says that it was "all kind of a blur."

A couple of years later, Terri got pregnant again. Wanting to protect the health of her unborn child coupled with her fear of her toddler catching her in the act of her behaviors, she finally forced herself to stop and take a look at what her relationship with her body might cost her. "When I decided to stop, I had a three-year-old at the time. Three-year-olds are curious, and three-year-olds follow you into the bathroom. I knew that it would be too traumatic if my child ever saw me making myself get sick; so, because of my kids, I knew that it wasn't going to work and that I didn't want to continue. The truth is that, if I had a place to escape, if I knew that I could send them off to play and go and do my thing, I probably would not have stopped. I just didn't have that option."

Over time, Terri was able to overcome the addictive pattern that the bulimia had become, all the while raising her kids, going through a divorce, working full time, and eventually remarrying. Reflecting back on it now, she can see the false sense of control and confidence that it gave her. "I am sure that people have all different reasons for having an eating disorder. I have always been an anxious person. For me, it reduced my anxiety, and it helped me to feel like I could look as good as I wanted to look as quickly as I could get there. I understand the psychological prison that an eating disorder is. I was a prisoner, too, and I have sympathy for those who are currently struggling. Nothing extreme is good: extreme eating, exercising, or drinking. I think that bulimia had such power over me because it gave me a sense of control over my body. Wrong. I had no control and am, thankfully, now free from those impulses."

As a professional, knowing the intense grip that is an eating disorder, I am amazed that Terri was able to stop the behaviors without outside intervention. Most who struggle require some type of professional intervention. The cessation of dangerous behaviors, while imperative for health, is, however, one part of the equation. Terri's lifelong struggle with her appearance, weight, and shape further illustrates the deep complexities of these issues for so many women. Body image issues are a part of life with an eating disorder. Body image issues drive women to engage in eating disorder behaviors. But, sadly, body dissatisfaction can linger long after eating disorder behavior is extinguished, and it can, of course, impact girls and women of all ages regardless of whether or not they engage in life threatening or dangerous habits.

In talking about the rift between how girls and women actually look and how they want to look, Terri shares "I would look at myself and then I would look at people that I thought looked really good, and I didn't look like them. During the time that I was growing up, there wasn't anything that said, 'You're good the way you are.' For me, it was a matter of, 'How would I like to look?' It was never going to happen for me naturally, because that wasn't my body type, my genetics. When I look back at pictures of me in college, I feel like I looked great. I felt like my clothing fit really well. I was so slender. The whole time, I was convinced that I was in control of it, that I wouldn't ever get to a point where I did damage to my body or my esophagus. I had heard that Karen Carpenter had died of an eating disorder, but I believed that I was impervious, that I would never get to that point. I thought that I was invincible. The whole thought about what it would do to my health didn't really enter my mind. How I looked was more important than my health—that and feeling a sense of control. I don't have control over the future, but, in those moments, I felt like I did. There were a lot of things in my life that I didn't have control over."

Now in her sixth decade of life, Terri believes that this is an issue for women of all ages, not just girls and young women, like so many falsely believe. She admits that she still has an intense concern over how she looks, and her deep concern about her weight has not diminished with age. "I compensate now by working out more and eating less. I work full time, and I nibble food throughout the day. I don't actually sit down and eat a meal most days. I don't tend to eat dinner a lot. I am always concerned about how I look."

In asking why she still cares, why it matters now that she is established in her career, having successfully raised her kids, and after finding a life partner, Terri replies, "I want people to think that I am attractive, I want my husband to be attracted to me, I want people to think that we are lucky to be together. It matters to me that I keep trying. It's a self-pressure. I can be very critical. I feel like I have to hold myself to a standard."

Terri says she has drawn the line at times over the years with the pressure that she puts on herself. She shares with me that she did decide at one point against getting a breast augmentation and that she has tried to discourage her daughter from getting plastic surgery. "This is me," she tells me.

Terri and her lifelong struggle reflect how our relationships with our bodies, health, exercise, nutrition and well-being can endure over time. "Would I call myself a recovered bulimic?

"I thought that I was invincible. The whole thought about what it would do to my health didn't really enter my mind. How I looked was more important than my health—that and feeling a sense of control. I don't have control over the future, but, in those moments, I felt like I did. There were a lot of things in my life that I didn't have control over."

It's not like it's out of my train of thought. But I no longer feel like I need to get rid of food. I just tell myself to eat a smaller portion and just really limit myself. I don't eat fast food and am very selective. But I don't think anymore about purging, and so, I'm happy that that part of my life is behind me. I'm happy with the way that I look. There are some parts that I know I'll never be able to change. It's not the 'perfect look' but that's me. It's okay. It helps when someone you love acknowledges you in a positive way. As much as it would be nice to feel like we don't need that outside affirmation, those things matter. I am now married to a wonderful man who tells me that I am beautiful. I'm at a normal weight, and I exercise regularly. I still don't eat really well, but am grateful for vitamins and for protein drinks (or I wouldn't have any hair)."

REFLECTION TIME

As you read Terri's story, what thoughts came to mind?

What are the "hang-ups, fears, or issues" about body image that you have that you hope to shed as you grow older?

Terri shares that her motivation to stop using harmful behaviors stemmed from wanting to protect her children. Are there loved ones in your life that you hope to be a role model for with more positive body image, self-esteem, and self-regard?

10

HELP

"Eating Disorders and Trauma"

"I think I need some help."

That's what I told my parents over the phone in the middle of the night while miles away from home during my sophomore year in college in 1997. I was on the floor in the bathroom. It was one of those moments when the tile should have felt colder than it actually was. I lived in the deep South at the time, where the only time a Midwestern-raised girl like me might feel cold was in the freezer section of the grocery store. In the months leading up to this phone call that surely awakened my then-frightened parents from their sleep, I had begun bingeing. Not just overeating. Truly bingeing. The kind that hurts. Badly. The amount of food that makes your insides ache and twist and wreaks havoc on your skin, your stomach, your mood, and completely zaps you of all of your energy. I had always loved food, but the part of me that had begun gorging was an unfamiliar beast. She was ravenous for something and, without knowing what it was, had turned to food to satiate the deep and intense hunger within.

The bingeing was a problem for sure, but the greater problem was when I began to try in earnest to get rid of that food by purging in the bathroom when my roommate was asleep or out of the apartment. I knew that I didn't want to go down that road. I knew that I needed help. So, in an act that I now see as heroic and life-changing, I called to ask for it.

My foray into purging was short-lived and, thankfully, mostly unsuccessful. The bingeing episodes, before I got a handle on them, were at times intense. My weight at that time was higher than my body's natural "set point" due to the increased caloric intake and the literal feeding frenzy for my unchecked emotions and my shame about the way that I felt and looked. Once I started therapy, I began to see patterns emerging. And I began to put the puzzle pieces together as to how to better control my coping and how to begin to see myself in an entirely new way.

Entering into therapy at that time in my life was truly a fork in the road. Without this intervention, I could have just gone down the path of trying to deal with feelings through behaviors, all the while keeping my sensitivities, my emotions, and my self-loathing buried deep inside. I didn't like the way that I felt, and I was realizing that I hadn't for a long time.

You would never have known it on the outside, with my outgoing personality and my busy, bustling social life. I had always had lots of friends—had always felt like I had a front-row seat "on the inside" of things. I had never felt overly depressed, except for the times that breakups made it glaringly obvious how easily I had handed over my entire heart without any thought about the possibility of it getting shattered to pieces. By the time I was nineteen, on the outside it looked like I had it all together. On the inside, however, I was fairly intense and needy, lacking in strong coping skills to deal with the stuff of life. Therapy was the doorway to beginning to explore all of this for me.

My journey into healing my relationship with myself required a good, hard look at things.

With the loving guidance and support of my therapist, I began to piece together how I had gotten to that low point on the bathroom floor. I began to see how feeling like I was overweight as a kid solidified a self-image and a corresponding story of my body that perpetuated over and over—in all kinds of ways that impacted my self-esteem. I began to see how the influence of diet culture in the '80s and early '90s had influenced me. And, for the first time, I began to question who I really was and what I was here to do.

By the time that I had graduated college, my confidence had started to blossom. A voice began to emerge. I found myself having spiritual and personal experiences that, to this day, have shaped my adult life. And yet, the arrival at some finished point on the journey never came. The reality is that there is no perfect version of recovery, life, or selfhood. Yes, I had learned some beautiful lessons, but it didn't mean that I arrived at some magical place where the struggle had dissipated into some blissful state of self-acceptance. It's as if all that time that I was building new muscles to combat the forces of negativity that would continue to threaten me, I just had new skills to employ when the time came to still come out victorious, in spite of being bloodied a bit from time to time even well into adulthood.

Everyone thinks that they know what it looks like to have an eating disorder. Everyone has a mental picture of an emaciated, young, white female; usually adolescent. The truth of the matter is that most girls and women that have clinical eating disorders do not fit that mold (eating disorders are on the rise in males as well). If you were to walk into any eating disorder treatment center, you would likely be shocked as to how "normal" the residents appeared to you. When we talk about eating disorders, there are the diagnoses that everyone thinks they "know" about, like anorexia nervosa and bulimia nervosa. But there's far more to it than just that. We now know that there are several types of eating disorders, including the lesser-talked-about binge eating disorder, and orthorexia, a clinical diagnosis describing the maladaptive pattern of disordered eating and self-image under the guise of being "healthy," "eating clean," and overexercising.

Eating disorders do not just affect one small segment of our population but, in fact, affect all races, genders, ages, and socioeconomic groups. Comorbid conditions such as depression, anxiety, PTSD, OCD, substance abuse, and many other mental health issues often go hand in hand with these disorders. Far from being manifested by only those who are young, thin, white girls just wanting to be "skinny," these situations involve all sorts of individuals with highly complex illnesses that are very difficult to successfully treat and require ongoing intervention in several areas of life, including nutrition therapy, psychiatry, and other modalities.

According to the National Association of Anorexia Nervosa and Associated Disorders, what is the number-one risk factor for developing an eating disorder?[5]

Body image issues.[5]

Paulina, age twenty-three, first realized that she had abnormal eating patterns when she was around ten or eleven years old. She remembers eating a large amount of food and recalls being called out not just for eating such "unhealthy" things but also for the amount that she was ingesting. Out of shame and embarrassment, she began to secretly hide food and then ate it in the bathroom, flushing wrappers down the toilet so as not to get caught. By sixth grade, she was not eating at all during the school day and was wearing the same baggy sweatshirt to avoid anyone seeing her body. All throughout middle school, she struggled until, in eighth grade, she began in earnest to try to lose weight, at first by exercising, then using laxatives, and finally, by high school, developing a deadly and intense pattern of bingeing and purging. The weight began to drop off, her "interest" in running at school intensified, and the compliments about how good she looked came in fast and furious. All came to a crashing halt when she was admitted to a treatment center where she spent two months before being sent to a therapeutic boarding school out of state for a year in order to stabilize her physical and mental health.

Paulina considers herself to be "on the right path" now, but admits to having moments of being self-conscious and judging her body and her food choices. When she does catch herself feeling negative, she forces herself to say five positive things about her body and what it does

"My body image issues can still be so extreme. Some days I feel attractive. Some days I have intense body dysmorphia. There can be days of intense self-loathing that are terrible, overwhelming, and really hard. Changing my perspective and self-talk can help, but it's a struggle, and it's hard to find a middle ground of acceptance."

— KATHERINE, 31

for her. She also reminds herself that "Every body is beautiful. Food is nourishment and the ultimate medicine for one's body."

The cost of having an eating disorder is high in just about every way. Often, these struggles can cost someone time, money, and resources to invest in a team-based treatment approach. They can rob someone of years of their life. And they can collectively rob the world of many gifts that are there to be shared, yet get put on a shelf—unable to compete with bandwidth that is already full by thinking of food, weight, and body image. For so many girls and women, these are literally years that they instead spend living inside a prison that only they have the key to release themselves from. And these are years that they can't get back.

Jenna is all-edges in all of the coolest ways. With a wicked style and undeniably striking physical features, her blue eyes are intensely captivating. She is a talented musician, incredibly smart, and seems like she can hang with all of the dudes while, at the same time, be the girl that all the girls want to be besties with. She is deep, complex, and has an aura that is undeniably compelling. While she frequently gets feedback along these lines, it often falls on deaf ears as she struggles to see herself in a way that is so incredibly obvious to the rest of the world.

Jenna reports that, around the age of nine or ten, she had some issues with her body right before puberty. Mild and inconsistent, her body wasn't something that she really thought much about in depth until around the age of fifteen. Up until that time, she saw her body 'as an instrument.' She was an active participant in sports and was already on her way to being a passionate and talented drummer. Around the ages of fifteen and sixteen, Jenna started to have some digestive issues and was put on a gluten-free diet. The need to eliminate so much from her diet and be careful in what she was eating resulted in an unintentional and significant weight loss from her naturally smaller frame. This seemingly "healthy" change in eating behavior unknowingly set in motion an eating disorder that she is still struggling to completely recover from fifteen years later.

As her teen years raged on, Jenna's weight loss started to "feel good." Too good. A pattern of restriction became ingrained. Despite weight loss and concern from parents and loved ones about looking "too thin," a distorted body image and a sense of feeling bigger and "fatter" than she actually was took hold of her psyche. Her academics and pursuit of her education took a back seat as these emerging body issues took hold in every way. Music went on the back burner, and her flagging energy and mental focus due to not eating enough had started to take a toll. At the age of sixteen, with her high school career and promising musical endeavors on the horizon, her life came to a grinding halt. Jenna ended up hospitalized at a local eating disorder inpatient recovery unit, with the hope and intention to get to the bottom of the increasingly distorted thinking and simultaneously uncontrolled weight loss. Years later, at thirty-one, Jenna laments the fact that the body image issues have continued to this day, ranging from "manageable, to unmanageable, to somewhere in between."

Jenna looks back on that first hospitalization and remembers herself as being "rebellious and angry." It was all new to her to have a "diagnosis," at the same time, she found herself not wanting to change what she was doing. In those early days, she felt that she received more concern than praise for the way that she looked; however the praise and attention that solidified the alliance with the disordered behavior came soon enough and endures to this day. "Looking back, I was highly resistant to treatment. At the time, I was pretty much forced to go through the motions of 'recovery,' even though I was not making any real changes to how I was thinking or what I was doing."

Treatment persisted and a diagnosis was made for a previously undiagnosed mood disorder. With the secondary diagnosis, medication was prescribed; and, from an emotional standpoint, treatment seemed to be progressing. "I was put on medication for my mood disorder and, for the first time, started to find a kind of stability. I gained a lot of weight on the medication, and I couldn't look at myself. I hated my body. But emotionally, I finally started to feel okay." A resulting additional diagnosis of ADD and an additional medication, which then resulted in another round of weight loss, unfortunately started the cycle all over again.

At this point, Jenna's physique began to earn her quite a bit of attention and praise. Reveling in the attention, and wearing outfits that revealed her body, Jenna reports having that thin body again "became like a drug." Like drugs in general, however, there are side effects. And consequences. While garnering attention for being "thin and beautiful," she managed to achieve society's all-consuming end game and life goal, only to find her life derailed and taken off course even further.

In her early twenties, Jenna found herself in another residential treatment center, still not wanting to change, but not able to sustain what was going on with her body and her health. Something, however, about this round of treatment started to feel different, and she began to think for the first time about recovery. At that point, she committed to several more months in that facility; and from there, she moved across the country to a sober-living and more long-term treatment program, where she worked hard to change her life over the course of several years. Slowly, over time, she finally began to recover lost pieces of herself outside of her appearance and weight and body. She began to see more aspects of who she is at the core and began, for the first time, to appreciate who she is.

After about three years of living away from home, Jenna moved back to her home state and began working in sales and living independently. Reconnecting with friends at that time has been lifesaving and crucial, as these friendships have seen her through her challenges over all of those years. She feels that the support of friends and family has been "everything" for her in coming home from treatment and trying to find her way.

Looking back on it now, Jenna describes how her personality, messages from her environment, and her mental health issues all hit at once "in a perfect storm"—one that hit hard and left her for dead. The eating disorder had come to serve a purpose in her life, in spite of knowing logically that it wasn't just about her body and that the way she looked "really doesn't matter." Engaging in all of those behaviors, achieving what society told her was "desirable," became like an addiction; one that, on some level, continues to be a part of her life all these years later.

"Hypersexualizaton of young girls concerns me the most. It teaches them that nipped, tucked, inflated, and sexualized is the standard. It creates unrealistic expectations and reinforces that their bodies are objects to be judged."

— MEGAN, 37

She admits that getting to know herself outside of her physical body and appearance has been complicated and hard. "It's human nature to want to do things that feel good. For me, it's to an extreme. It's innately ingrained to take it to a degree that's not healthy."

When asked about the degree to which this obsession and disorder has held her back and affected the trajectory of her life, Jenna says, "It has 100 percent impacted my life in every way. It has delayed my ability to find myself, my music. Who knows where I could be if I had been doing that and how different my life could be and how many years that I could have reveled in that? I lost that time. But there are also parts of this journey that I don't necessarily regret. There are a lot of qualities, like resilience, that I have learned through all of this. I have lost some things for sure. But it has also fueled what I am working toward now and what I do like about myself." Dealing with those losses now at thirty-one years old is a bitter pill to swallow. But she now looks forward with hope and optimism about the ability to impact the world and free herself once and for all with the shift to more bandwidth for who she is here to be.

"My dad and I were talking about life when I was in a dark place recently. He told me, 'Your number one goal should be to be happy.' It sounds so obvious and so cliche, but it wasn't to me. I have been trying to shift my focus more onto the qualities of me that make me 'me,' that are really cool, and that don't have anything to do with how much money I make or how I look. It's not what I value. It's just that simplest thing. That's really all I want. Maybe I thought that reaching for that stuff would make me happy, but it doesn't. Music makes me happy. Helping people makes me happy."

As women develop, there are a myriad of pitfalls that can detour healthy body image and self-worth. Eating disorders are one of them. In addition to that, though, are the very real issues of trauma, and an ongoing confusion about the mixed messages we receive in society about female sexuality. Trauma is shattering to the core. The effects of sexual trauma are so deep and so severe, and yet it is still something that, in spite of the recent Me Too Movement, lives in the deep and dark shadows of the body, the mind, and the heart for many, many girls and women.

Overcoming sexual trauma and the ramifications on the relationship to self and others can take years, and it often requires professional intervention.

The confusing and mixed messages about sexuality for our girls bombards them at younger and younger ages. Skimpy and provocative clothing is marketed to young girls as the beauty and diet industry constantly chime in to remind girls that being attractive is their top priority. Girls and young women are hypersexualized by society, and then, simultaneously shamed for the overt use of their bodies to gain some amount of status, attention, or power (although, this difference in messaging often comes from varying groups with different values and beliefs). Then, as women age, they are seen as increasingly less sexy and attractive. At middle age, a time in life when many women finally begin to settle into their relationships to self in a deeper and more positive way, the voices outside of themselves can work to render them disconnected from and devoid of any sense of sensuality and sexuality. These messages. These issues. No wonder why women's relationships with their bodies are so complex, so fraught with deep, painful layers that need to safely and carefully be excavated and released.

In spite of the reality of these issues, help and hope is available. Many women have recovered from eating disorders, trauma, and sexual abuse. And many of them would affirm that ultimately finding peace and stability is worth the fight. True healing comes when courage and vulnerability grow seeds that blossom into empowerment, recovery, and change. And the true beauty of that is undeniable.

——————— LET'S TALK! ———————

Educate yourself about eating disorders. Know the warning signs and the behaviors that indicate that you or someone you love may need professional help. You can learn more from the National Association for Anorexia Nervosa and Associated Disorders at ANAD.org.

Spend some time questioning what you have internalized about sexuality and your body. If you or someone you know has been the victim of sexual trauma, reach out and get help.

CONCLUSION

who are you here to be?

"I am forty-five and a fierce feminist and activist who is spending much of her day thinking not about the revolution or Other Human Beings, but about the three brownies that I ate last night and if those three brownies somehow changed the trajectory of my life and proved that I am, in fact, after all . . . Bad!!!!!"[6]

———————————————

The above was an Instagram post written by Glennon Doyle early in January in 2021. Doyle is not only a best-selling author multiple times over but also a podcast powerhouse and an incredible voice for change and activism in the world. Words that have been used to describe the impact of her books and her work in the world are life-changing, game-changing, wildly inspiring, and exactly what I needed to hear. She has persevered through addiction, and has spoken honestly about her relapses with mental health and bulimia, admitting that she still struggles herself with issues of food and body image. She is outspoken, motivating, and courageous . . . and, apparently, still sometimes rendered powerless and overwhelmed by the act of eating a few brownies.[6]

When I read her vulnerable and honest post, instantly my thoughts were, "Wait, what? That woman? That force of nature? That incredible embodiment of good and change and power in the world? Are we talking about the woman that lifts other women up so incredibly high that they see themselves from an entirely new altitude? She is stressing about a few brownies?!?"

Yes.

Because, as women, our intense issues, insecurities, vulnerabilities and shame about food and our bodies are that pervasive. Are that insidious. Are that deeply embedded in the way that we feel about ourselves.

According to Brené Brown, famed author and psychological researcher, the number one source of shame and vulnerability for women is their bodies and the way that they look. Their bodies. And the way that they look.

These waters run deep. We are all steeped in it. We brine in it.

Jackie says that she became aware of her body image around age twelve. It started with what she describes as an "acne problem"; and, looking back, she remembers that she didn't even want to go to school because she felt "ugly." Jackie was raised in a small, predominantly black community in the South, and says that, for women of her race, looking good is all about having curves—"breasts and a backside!" As her body began to develop, it was clear to her that she was going to be tall and naturally thin, and she constantly battled how differently her body looked compared to the other girls in her community. In addition to her body and her acne, Jackie says that she had problems with her teeth that she didn't fix until adulthood, leaving her feeling "not good enough," "not pretty enough," and often trying hard not to smile. Looking back, she says she felt "miserable."

"I was never comfortable with who I was. Because I was so focused on my outer appearance, I just couldn't focus on other goals, like college and what else I could do with my life. It was obsessive for me. I was smart, but I felt like I wasn't going to do anything because of how I looked." She says she often compared herself to her friends and other girls in her neighborhood. "All the girls were developing and looking good, and I thought they were all so beautiful. I was just so overwhelmed. At that time, there were no role models. None of the older women in the community talked about their bodies or our bodies. My mother was an alcoholic, and she always was saying negative things. No one was talking to us and guiding us. I feel like things would have been different for me if they had."

When Jackie was in her twenties and thirties, having suffered for a long time with her self-esteem, she says that she found herself trying to give other girls what she didn't have and knew she had needed while growing up. "I would find myself telling younger girls, 'It's not about your body. It's not about that eyeshadow or all of that makeup. This is what makes you beautiful. This is what makes you smart. It's what lies inside of you. What goals do you have? What do you want to be? What are you going to do tomorrow?' " These are the things that she would talk about with the girls. She further explains, "I didn't have that, and I feel like it made a difference in the lives of those women."

Jackie credits God and her father for helping her turn the tide on her issues with her self-worth and her body image. "My father pushed me and showed me love. He told me that I was beautiful and that I was smart. He was my driving force. I looked at my mother, and I said, 'I'm going to show you what a woman should be.' I just had that drive to be the woman and the mother that she should have been, and I decided that I was going to show her how it's done. And I was going to do it with grace."

While Jackie had reached what felt like a turning point, there were still several decades of challenges and obstacles that she had to work to overcome. Her first marriage ended in her forties. "My ex-husband was negative. He would talk negatively about everything that I did and everything that I said, because he was trying to keep me down." She says that she knew that if she was focusing on all of the negativity and the way she looked, she wasn't going to get anywhere. "I knew that I had to focus on something else other than what I looked like." Over the course of her life, Jackie has set her feet upon the path to improving her self-love and confidence, but she has also grieved the loss of a daughter and battled mental health issues with her son that have left him estranged to her now. Working through those challenges as well as remarrying, Jackie feels that, at least in terms of her body and appearance, she has finally come to a place of "peace." She says, "I feel free. I feel less pressure now. After all I have been through, I have decided that I just can't stress over things. I am going to go into retirement, and I want to be happy and healthy. I have a choice. I am taking the high road."

When describing her version of self-acceptance, Jackie clearly expressed, "I could look at myself and say, 'There's a lot of things I need to fix or change.' But I'm a sixty-two-year-old woman! I exercise. I try not to stress out. I keep my body in good shape. But the other stuff? I just let it happen. I'll throw on a little makeup, and I'm good. I don't care. I have beautiful legs. I know that I'm not too bad to look at! Also, people love me because of me! I know that I've got some other stuff going on inside of me. People gravitate toward me because we have good conversations. I'm a good person. I am the soul that lies within."

When asked about what she would tell her younger self now, with her perspective of her wisdom, Jackie says, "I would tell my younger self to spend all of my time and energy on my higher calling, instead of focusing on what I look like, because you are called to something. Let that be your light. Spend all of that time and energy on that, because that is where your rewards are going to be, and that is where your beauty lies."

Girls. Women. Our culture. Our bodies. Our relationships with food and exercise. Comparisons. The negative talk amongst each other. The negative talk within ourselves. The teen years. Pregnancy. Midlife and beyond. It's all so complex. So layered. When it comes both to body image and life in general, no one is perfect. No one is nailing it. No one has all of life and themselves figured out. While this struggle can feel so universal—and, in a lot of ways it is—we are also all so unique in our own stories and issues and perspectives.

It's time to stop chasing perfection. There is no perfect body. There is no perfect relationship to food. We need to make a commitment to let go of perfectionism in all areas and do the best that we can. And that first starts by busting all of the myths and stories that society sells us about this elusive perfection that we are paying the price for in our blood, sweat, tears, and souls. Let's take away the "good" or "bad" labels when it comes to our bodies, our foods, and ourselves. That was the old game. We get to make up our own rules now about who we want to be, what we like, and what we do.

Yes, I have a master's degree in clinical social work. Yes, I have been an "expert" in this field for almost twenty years. But I call the bluff on anyone who is out there saying that they have it all figured out. I am human too. Over the years, I have been in and out of therapy when I need it. I work at self-love and acceptance daily. I am committed to doing the work, because there is always work to be done. The longer that I am on this planet, the more that I listen to and talk to women, the more that I believe that, no matter who you are, if you are female and breathing, you have a complicated story about your body. That story is likely a complex brew of shame, pride, guilt, sexuality, deprivation, pleasure, confusion, love, hate, angst, and gratitude. And that story is mine too.

Media, social media, messages and stories from childhood, incredible forces of patriarchy or matriarchy, gender stereotypes, power struggles, and manipulation—it's the continuous chorus about how women don't measure up, aren't good enough, aren't beautiful enough, aren't thin enough, or aren't doing enough. And it's all at fever pitch. They are shouting and screaming at us, and we are not deaf and cannot be immune and most of us have internalized these messages for a long, long time. But we can start to talk back. In fact, we can and should shout back. Fight back. Stand our ground and vow to neither swallow nor spread the poison any more. Find and take the high ground.

"I think that every woman should embrace her diversity. We are all beautiful and confident in our own ways, and that is what makes us unique. Without diversity and differences, everything would be boring. Embrace your differences, and remain confident in who you are. Most importantly, be unapologetically yourself."

— LAUREN, 19

As women, it's time to take back the conversation. We have to change how we talk about other women and to other women and to our girls and to ourselves. And it is going to be hard. It's going to be hard because we have to start unlearning some things. What we have learned is deeply ingrained and embedded. It will require us to be gentle with ourselves. It will require us to be compassionate with ourselves. We need new tools to deal with our insecurities. New insights and awareness. It takes time to develop new behaviors, beliefs, patterns, narratives, and stories. But I know that we can do it. And I know that we can do it together—because that is what women do and have always done. We are our own tribe within the tribe, and we are fierce and powerful and determined. We can start now to stand up for ourselves and each other and rise together.

So, let's all agree. Let's agree to stop talking with our girlfriends about whose body part we want. Let's stop comparing ourselves and each other. Let's stop sharing those memes. Let's stop body shaming ourselves and others. Let's stop worrying about our extra "weight" or our daughter's extra "weight." Instead of worrying about how society is going to judge us or our daughters based on our appearance, let's be the loudest and the fiercest and most dominant voice that a superficial society does not have the right to define our worth and our value based on how we look or what we weigh. Let's stop trying to control our lives by forcing our bodies to conform. Let's stop buying into the myth that, in order to transform our lives, we have to first transform our bodies.

Famed poet Mary Oliver asks, "Tell me, what is it you plan to do with your one wild and precious life?"[7] And so I ask you, "What is your plan to care for and love your one wild and precious body that carries you through this one wild and precious life? How are you going to treat it?" Because we only get one. No matter what society wants us to believe, we cannot control it. Yes, we can care for it. We can tend to it. We can rest it and feed it and move it and love it. But we cannot control it. And it's time to stop feeling like we should have to. It's time to stop believing in the seductive and false myth of the "transformation of our bodies." Much of physical transformation being promoted is only skin deep. What the world so desperately needs now is the transformation of women that is soul deep. This planet and our kids need the transformation of girls and women that far transcends our outward shell of our physical appearance and shines forth something ultimately so much more powerful. So much more beautiful. So much more courageous and braver and whole.

In order to do this, we all need to agree to change the conversation. Centuries of cultural expectations and the suppression of women may have created this tangled mess, but unraveling and undoing this mess is our work alone. Women need to take back our power, stand in the full measure of it, and then wield it with all of our might. It's time to take this negativity out of circulation. It's time for women to define what we think is beautiful. On our terms. We live in a world so full of mind-boggling beauty and diversity. It is dizzying and endless. And there is a place for all of us to stand in the light of what is seen as beautiful. Women have such incredible talents, gifts, and wisdom. We have lost sight of that. And the world needs us to see this in ourselves and needs us to do the work that we are all here to do.

I have often asked my clients in therapy to reflect on their deepest-held, most true, and most meaningful values. There is something very powerful about asking someone to assess and reflect on how they want to be remembered and what they will have given toward their life purpose. What do they want others who walked in life with them to remember about them? In almost twenty years of doing this work, no one has ever said, "I want people to know me most for how pretty I am," or "I want to be remembered for how fit or thin I was." Even my clients who struggle the most with body image, self-esteem, and self-image will say that their external appearance doesn't really align with their most meaningful values in life.

Who are we here to be? What are our values? What are we here to do? It's okay if the answers to those questions change over time. It's okay if the answers to those questions aren't big, life-altering, or game-changing on a global scale. It's okay if we don't even have the answers to those questions. But it is important to keep asking them.

This is the stuff that matters. And it all matters. Each of us and what we do on a daily basis in the spirit of love, service, and offering up our own unique gifts matter. Whatever you can do today, big or small, do that. With all of your heart and all of your might. Nothing is insignificant. It's all ripples. And to make those ripples add up to more ripples, which will then add up to waves; we are all going to have to leave behind our beliefs and our stories that we are "not good enough."

We also need to be mindful of extending grace and love to all women, no matter how they choose to live their lives. Whether they embrace fitness, dress a certain way, or decide to get cosmetic surgery, everyone is on their own path and doing the best that they can. Amanda, age twenty-five, talks about how making the decision to get a breast augmentation helped her let go of unhealthy behaviors by finally helping her feel confident in a way that she doesn't know she could have attained without taking that step. "Growing up, I was actually known for and teased for having small boobs. Even my best friend would comment about it when we were shopping. I took it as an insult, and I became so fixated on that. I became so unhappy with my body. I felt like a boy. I felt like my body was so mismatched, and I didn't feel feminine. I did get a breast augmentation, and I don't regret that. I feel content with my body now, and I think a lot of my confidence comes from that. It might be narcissistic to say, and I don't think everyone should get plastic surgery, but for me, it made me feel better. After that point, I stopped with the diets and the constant working out."

What works for one will not work for all. Kathleen, fifty-seven years old, agrees, "We also need to accept and love those women that do make the choice to get plastic surgery, to color their hair, to get liposuction. We need to stop judging. If a woman is sixty years old and wants to put on a full face of makeup, God love her, she should go for it. If you are naturally a size two, great! Let's celebrate it. The grace that we need to remember to extend to ourselves, we need to remember to extend it to everyone else as well. Don't shame other women. We are all in this together. Gone are the glass ceilings of yesteryear. There is no limit to our abilities. We all have the same mountain to climb."

We are all on our own journeys. My journey, too, has been complicated and challenging to eventually land in a place of self-love and acceptance. Personally, I like makeup and fashion. I choose to focus on health and wellness. I enjoy working out. I like social media. I engage in these things because they add value and meaning and creativity and beauty and inspiration into my life. But I do not obsess over them. They do not define me. They do not define what I am here to do. Who I am here to be. I am here to be a spiritual being, a wife, a mother, a helper, a creative, an artist, a daughter, a sister, an aunt, and a friend. I am here to use my voice and my gifts and my talents for the greater good. And I cannot and will not let the trappings of how I look or how much I weigh get in the way of who I am here to be.

Learning to love our bodies, for so many of us, may just mean loving them in spite of not totally and always loving the way that they look. Self-love may mean just committing to taking care of our bodies, in spite of the things that we wish we could change about their outward appearance. It is about acceptance of—being okay with the way things are—rather than what our culture trains us to wish that they could be.

It's difficult. I, myself, do not do this perfectly every day. But I no longer believe in perfection. I do the best that I can, given the hardwiring that society gave me that I am constantly working to rewire. It's hard work. But we women are used to doing hard work.

With all that still needs to change in order for women to see and embrace their own beauty inside and out, in the end, I am hopeful. I am hopeful that the women of this book, and all of the voices out there, are changing the conversation. It would seem as if the message is ever so slowly getting through. It would seem as if girls and women are waking up to this realization that they are in charge of their own stories, their own narratives, their own power.

Oh, and one more thing—what about Michelle Obama's arms?

Do I wish that I had them? I don't know. Maybe. Would my life be any different if I did have them? Probably not. For me, the true measure of what I aspire to in other women has less to do with how they look and more to do with what they embody, what they stand for, and the spirit that flows through them. I am willing to bet that Michelle Obama does not want her legacy to be how fit and toned her arms looked in a designer dress on her husband's inauguration night. I am willing to bet that the legacy that is most important to Michelle Obama, her girls, her loved ones, and the world, is her dignity. Her grace. Her leadership. Her tenacity. Her strength as a woman. Who she is here to be and what she is here to do.

Compare, and you get despair. Change the conversation. Be who you are here to be, in all of its unique and gorgeous glory.

——————— LET'S TALK! ———————

Develop an "attitude of gratitude" about your body. What gifts has your body given you? What does it allow you to do?

Reverse the Golden Rule. Treat yourself the way that you would treat others. Most women and girls struggle with incredibly high standards and judgments that they would never impose on anyone else. Give yourself the same respect that you so graciously give away.

Manage your self-talk. Pay attention to the things that you say and think about yourself, your food, your weight, and your appearance.

When you get stuck focusing on how you look or what you weigh, ask yourself instead, "Who am I here to be today?"

Find something that you like about your physical self and show it off. Highlight it. Be proud of it.

Embrace your own unique style and gifts.

Free up bandwidth that is taken up by counting calories, worrying about food, hating your body, or comparing yourself to others. I have heard some girls and women say that they spend upwards of 70 to 90 percent of their waking hours thinking about food, weight, and appearance. How else could you use that time and energy?

Make new habits:

- Throw away the scale.
- Stop dieting. Don't count calories.
- Know your "why" for exercising.
- Strive for balance and moderation in all things.
- Model healthy body image.
- Let go of perfection.
- Accept those things about you that you cannot change.
- Move on. Life is too short not to.

Get clear on your values. Write them down. Refer back to them on days when your appearance or weight seems to be the highest priority.

Don't be afraid to ask for help, whether that's from a trusted friend, a family member, a spouse, a doctor, or a therapist. You do not have to go it alone, ever.

ENDNOTES

"Dove Self-Esteem Project," Dove US, Dove.com, April 8, 2020, https://www.dove.com/us/en/dove-self-esteem
-project.html. Accessed April 13, 2022.

"The Success of Dove's Real Beauty Campaign," Global Brands Magazine, Global Brands Publications Limited,
February 9, 2022, https://www.globalbrandsmagazine.com/the-success-of-doves-real-beauty-campaign/. Accessed April 13, 2022.

"Reverse Selfie," Dove Global Channel, @Dove, Instagram, April 20, 2021, https://www.instagram.com/p
/CN4WowEHgxT/?hl=en. Accessed April 13, 2022.

Quote by Tracy Anderson, "TA Live Virtual Streaming Classes," Tracy Anderson Method, Tracy Anderson.com,
https://tracyanderson.com/category/press/.

National Association of Anorexia Nervosa and Associated Disorders, https://anad.org/get-informed/body-image/body
-image-articles/. Accessed June 3, 2022.

Doyle, Glennon [@glennondoyle], Instagram, January 2021. Accessed January 2021.

Oliver, Mary, "Poem 133: The Summer Day," Library of Congress, LOC.gov, https://www.loc.gov/programs/poetry-and
-literature/poet-laureate/poet-laureate-projects/poetry-180/all-poems/item/poetry-180-133/the-summer-day/.
Accessed May 11, 2022.

REVIEW INQUIRY

Hey, it's Gina here.

I hope that you've enjoyed the book, finding it both thought-provoking and inspiring. I have a favor to ask you.

Would you consider giving it a rating wherever you bought it? Online book stores are more likely to promote a work when they feel good about its content, and reader reviews are a great barometer for a book's quality.

So, please go to the website of wherever you bought the book, search for my name and the book title, and leave a review. If able, perhaps consider adding a picture of you holding the book. That increases the likelihood your review will be accepted!

Many thanks in advance,

Gina

WILL YOU SHARE THE LOVE?

Get this book for a friend, associate, or family member!

If you have found this book valuable and know others who would find it useful, consider buying them a copy as a gift. Special bulk discounts are available if you would like your whole team or organization to benefit from reading this work. Just contact GinaMichelleG@icloud.com or visit www.LifeLensAndLove.com.

WOULD YOU LIKE GINA GRAHAM TO SPEAK TO YOUR ORGANIZATION?

Book Gina now!

Gina accepts a limited number of speaking engagements each year. To learn how you can bring her message to your organization, contact Gina at GinaMichelleG@icloud.com or www.LifeLensAndLove.com.

ABOUT THE AUTHOR

Gina D. Graham is a licensed clinical social worker who has specialized in eating disorders, body image, depression, anxiety, and women's issues for twenty-plus years. Gina's private practice is located outside of Chicago.

In addition to her clinical work, Gina is a photographer specializing in portraiture of girls and women. Gina is passionate about showing women their true beauty and helping them see both their inner and outer selves through a new lens.

Gina is also a wife, a proud soccer mom, and a dog mom. She loves coffee and anything chocolate, and she refills her cup by traveling as much as she can.

For more info about Gina Graham, LCSW, and to follow along on her blog or Instagram or to inquire about speaking engagements, visit www.LifeLensAndLove.com or find her on social media @LifeLensAndLove.

Made in the USA
Middletown, DE
04 April 2023

28202559R00113